New Directions
in Religion and Aging

New Directions
in Religion and Aging

David B. Oliver, PhD
Editor

The Haworth Press
New York • London

New Directions in Religion and Aging has also been published as *Journal of Religion & Aging*, Volume 3, Numbers 1/2, Fall/Winter 1986.

The Haworth Press, Inc., 12 West 32 Street, New York, NY 10001
EUROSPAN/Haworth, 3 Henrietta Street, London WC2E 8LU England

Library of Congress Cataloging-in-Publication Data

New directions in religion and aging.

"Journal of religion & aging, volume 3, number 1/2."
Includes bibliographies.
1. Aged—Religious life. 2. Church work with the aged. I. Oliver, David B.
BV4580.N48   1987   261.8'3426   87-8557
ISBN 0-86656-553-1

New Directions in Religion and Aging

Journal of Religion & Aging
Volume 3, Numbers 1/2

CONTENTS

78233

ABOUT THE EDITOR

David B. Oliver, PhD, holds the Oubri A. Poppele Chair in Gerontology and Health and Welfare Studies at Saint Paul School of Theology in Kansas City, Missouri. His doctoral work (in sociology and gerontology) was completed at the University of Missouri in Columbia with a fellowship from the Midwest Council for Social Research in Aging. He has chaired the Departments of Sociology at the School of the Ozarks in Point Lookout, Missouri, and at Trinity University in San Antonio, Texas. In Texas, David was also an Adjunct Professor at the University of Texas Health Science Center (Medical School) and served on the Texas State Board of Licensure for Nursing Home Administrators. At Saint Paul, he has established a specialization in gerontology at both the Master of Divinity and Doctor of Ministry levels. All students at the seminary receive special training connecting ministry and aging. An experiential "hands-on" approach is his style. In "The World of Nursing Homes" class, for example, he and his students spend long hours in wheelchairs, gerichairs, and occasionally spend 24 hours in the nursing home as residents. Serving on the Certification Committee (two terms) for the American College of Health Care Administrators, he has helped establish professional standards beyond state nursing home licensure requirements. David has received a number of awards for outstanding teaching in the fields of gerontology and long term care. He is well known for his contributions to the field of aging and is clearly committed to improving the quality of life for persons of all ages.

PART I: NEW DIRECTIONS

Introduction

What an ambitious task, this predicting the future. When I first agreed to assemble a collection of articles on new directions in religion and aging, I thought what fun, what an opportunity to bring together some of the exciting minds from around the country and ask them to speculate on things to come in the next fifty years. Little did I realize how this would profoundly affect each one of them, both professionally and personally. The contributors to this enterprise were challenged to assess not only what perspectives their individual disciplines might offer, but they were confronted by their own aging as well. The authors quickly realized they were writing and prognosticating their own futures. They discovered that this was not an exercise involving strangers in a strange land, but rather that they were predicting what they will encounter as they move further down the life course.

Perhaps it is the relevance of this material to the writers' themselves which makes this work so much alive. While some view the future by looking at present trends, others look to the past, and still others call for a revolutionary approach to new possibilities. Part I, the first half of this effort, begins by setting aside some of the journalistic stereotypes and popular myths about aging. In fact, several articles confirm the observation made by James Thorson and Bruce Horacek that the plight of older persons in the future may be worse,

1

not better. They call for an intentional ministry which will address feelings of self-esteem, a sense of value, and the identities of the future elderly.

W. Paul Jones, in his comprehensive and reflective piece on theology and aging in the 21st century, connects a number and variety of variables in constructing a view of the elderly which moves from the future to the present. He challenges us all to consider our faith within the context of a dynamic and changing world. And in the end, it will be the elder theologians confronted by the reality of death, he claims, who will understand best the connection between religion and aging.

While Paul Jones, and others in this volume, see a relationship between aging and the process of death and dying, Robert E. Buxbaum suggests that the two should be considered as separate issues. He emphasizes the growing need for religious communities to be more responsive to the ubiquitous needs of the well-elderly who disproportionately dominate congregations. Toward this end, he advocates more intentional training of religious professionals in group process, in conflict resolution, and exposure to a theology of grace rather than works.

Biomedical ethics is indeed on everyone's list of present and future concerns. Health care in the United States is increasingly a system which must respond to an aging population, and Carl Chambers, Kathryn Pribble and Michael Harter paint a rather grim picture of possible outcomes for the elderly in the next fifty years. They provide evidence showing that the elderly's access to health care resources will become more restricted and that older persons will be placed at higher levels of risk.

The Chambers, Pribble and Harter paper also raises the issue of euthanasia and the right to die. Lindsey P. Pherigo brings the subject of inevitable death full circle. He suggests a few changes will occur in terms of where people will die, and sees little change in how natural death is understood, but he ("with considerable hesitation") calls for greater respect of the untouched area of investigation which has been created by discoveries in the new physics. He says, "It has made us aware that matter and energy are different forms of the same reality, and that space and time are not different qualitatively but are on a continuum. Physics has begun to document what imaginative science fiction writers have previsioned. We are now forced to acknowledge the limitations of human perceptions, and that the 'real world' is much larger than the part we can perceive."

Preoccupation with death is perhaps one theme which has attracted the attention of every generation since the beginning of time. W. Paul Jones, in his second contribution to this volume, makes a convincing case linking modern attitudes toward older persons (i.e., ageism) to the propensity for human denial and avoidance of the realities of death. He boldly and systematically debunks eight popular theories about aging, and using historical data, predicts that elders are, for most of us, symbolic reminders of death. The result, he claims, is a generalized rejection and departmentalization of older persons in our culture. We, in short, render them invisible. This historical trend, he suggests, will not reverse anytime soon.

An appropriate end to Part I is the contribution by Earl Brewer. He provides a useful theoretical framework from which to pose a number and variety of researchable questions which cry out for answers. His review of the literature in religion and aging demonstrates that the surface has barely been scratched, and this in spite of the recognized importance of religion in the lives of the elderly. If a sufficient number of "scholars and dollars" will focus on these exciting questions, the field of religion and aging may be well on its way to an established discipline in its own right.

Each author was invited to participate in this work because of previous academic and professional experience in specific areas of expertise. Questions and potential answers about the future did not come, however, without considerable struggle and reflection. One can look very bright and intelligent by interpreting the past, but one can be proven very wrong by the realities of the future. Thus I appreciate the boldness of these contributors as they held very little back in predicting the course of aging and the response to it by those in the religious sector of our society.

David B. Oliver, PhD
Editor

Self-Esteem, Value, and Identity: Who Are the Elderly, Really?

James A. Thorson, EdD
Bruce J. Horacek, PhD

SUMMARY. We may be more informed by journalistic stereotypes than by facts about the population of the aged. While older people of the future may be better educated and more prosperous, many may also be more isolated and frail. Happy mythology to the contrary, a good many aged people presently lead a marginal existence. We can anticipate a much greater number of fragile, lonely people in future years. The authors argue that intervention requires an intentional ministry to the isolated elderly.

Looking into the future can be a frustrating enterprise, particularly when we realize that many major social forces evolve only gradually, while others seem to change a population's values almost overnight. Influences like major wars or depressions are most difficult to predict, and the resultant changes from these influences are even more difficult to prophesy. To complicate things further, we seem to be only too eager to be informed by journalists like Toffler and Naisbitt, rather than taking a critical look at what really is going on around us.

Social change may be both rapid and glacial at the same time. Certainly few observers of the lunch counter sit-ins at Greensboro in 1963 would have predicted that a city like Atlanta would have a black mayor by 1976. Many of those who were critical of Adlai Stevenson's presidential candidacy in 1952 — he'd been divorced — lived to see divorce dwindle to a non-issue by the time Ronald Reagan ran for the presidency in 1980.

James A. Thorson is Professor and Director, and Bruce J. Horacek is Associate Professor and Academic Coordinator, Gerontology Program, University of Nebraska at Omaha, Omaha, Nebraska 68182.

5

Conversely, basic social structures in our society have changed little. People still live in families, care for their elders, are concerned for their children, and compete with their neighbors. While some may be taking on new roles, basic nurturing functions have remained pretty much the same. In the field of aging, we have seen more older people being able to afford an independent household, but the great majority still live near at least one adult child and look to that child as a primary caregiver. Thus, while details may have changed, the basic pattern has remained the same as it has been for at least several thousand years, and will likely be the same in the future.

Our task is to speculate, then, on how social and technological changes that we might anticipate will influence the older person of the future, and what the implications of this might be. Older people of the 20th century have seen rapid change going on around them. What changes will be influential, and which will only change the details? More specifically, how will future developments influence self-esteem, value, and identity among the elderly? Who will the older people of the future be, really?

HOW OLD IS OLD?

Our definition of old age, at the very basic level, probably will not change too much. Popular mythology to the contrary, our expectation of how old one needs to be in order to be an older person has changed very little over the centuries, nor will it change much in the future. The author of Psalm 90 described the length of life: three score and ten or four score by reason of strength. Three thousand years later we have pretty much the same rule of thumb: How old is old? Seventy or eighty.

Here is an area where the scholar must be on guard against the popular misinterpretations of would-be social historians. Many are only too eager to say that life in the future will be different "because people are living longer and longer." In fact, while it is true that average life expectancy has been increased—largely because of a decline in infant mortality, thus raising the average for the entire group—the anticipated life span itself has hardly changed at all. This simple fact is confused on a regular basis both by popular writers as well as those who should know better.[1] More people are surviving infancy and childhood so they have the chance to live out their allotted years, but the limit of those allotted years hasn't changed too much.

This is an area of real social change, but the observer needs to exercise particular caution not to jump on some journalistic bandwagon and misinterpret what in fact is going on. One of the genuine social revolutions of the 20th Century is that most people (about 73 percent of males and 84 percent of females) now live at least to age 65. At the beginning of the century, only about 38 percent of males and 43 percent of females lived to celebrate their 65th birthday.[2] On the other hand, those who were 65 in the year 1984 could anticipate only five years more of life than could the 65 year-old in 1900 (16.9 additional years, as compared to 11.9). In other words, more people are living into late life, but life-extending technologies have been of benefit mostly to the young, rather than to the old.

The implication of this is that there are more older people around, not that older people themselves are living much longer. It also means the emergence, as Fries and Crapo have observed, of universal chronic illness.[3] Fewer young people are dying of acute conditions, which means that more older people are dying of chronic conditions. Tuberculosis no longer kills young people; they now live long enough to die of heart disease and cancer.

One offshoot of this revolution in public health is that our image of death has changed during the present century. It is no longer a bolt out of the blue that carries off one's children; it is a gradual wasting process that finally provides a release for one's grandparents.

This demographic revolution, however, may have negative consequences in terms of value and self-esteem among the aged. Comparatively few people made up the population of the elderly in 1900; about four percent of the total were 65+. Presumably, there was some element of reverence or at least respect for the aged because they were fairly unique. Almost one out of five will be in the 65+ age group by the year 2025.[4] Few will receive any particular notice because of great age; it will be fairly common. There may well be less value placed on people who are no longer unique, and who may in fact be seen as a drag on the economy. Further, the popular stereotype of elders from an agrarian past having skills no longer of value in a highly technological age may have some basis in truth.

We have predicted, though, that the older person of the future will hardly fit the stereotype of the elderly of the past.[5] We have seen the image emerging of the healthy, prosperous, educated, active older person. No doubt these trends will continue. We certainly have no expectation of seeing older persons as psychological drop-outs whose circuits have frizzed from a rapidly accelerating pace of change. Older people are the masters of adaptation across the life span, and we see no evidence as to why this should change in the future.

However, this happy picture of a bright and shining old age for the majority may have less truth for a substantial minority of the elderly. Another demographic fact that we tend to forget is that the fastest-growing segment of our society is and will be the population 85 + .[6] That group — about two and a half million in 1983 — will have essentially doubled in size by the end of the present century. It will have almost doubled again by 2030 and again redoubled by the year 2050. Middle-level projections of population change from 1980 to 2030 see the population of the United States as a whole increasing by about 34 percent, but the number of those 85 + increasing by 279 percent.[6] These very old people, who represent less than one percent of the whole now, will comprise over five percent of the population in the year 2050. And, they are precisely the group that has most of the problems usually associated with old age.

HAPPY MYTHOLOGY – GRIM REALITY?

The field of gerontology is not so young that it has not developed its own orthodoxy. One of the most common educational goals of academic gerontologists has been to "demythologize" aging, to break down popularly-held stereotypes that old people are sick, poor, unhappy, and institutionalized. Despite these efforts, however, the vision of aging held by the general public is fairly negative. Klemmack and his colleagues[7] reviewed studies on the knowledge level of the public concerning aging and came to the dismal conclusion that not only is the knowledge level low, but most people tend to define the living conditions of older persons as worse than they actually are. Our own research[8] found that the younger the respondent, the more negative the attitude toward aging. The Lou Harris organization[9] again found both a high level of misunderstanding about old age and perceptions that the problems of older people were worse than those actually reported by the aged.

One is forced to ask why these negative images of aging persist. A simple, if heretical, explanation might be that a good many older people are in fact miserable. That is, despite the orthodoxy of the field — the majority of the aged are living happy, independent lives outside of institutions — it may also be true that a significant minority are sick, poor, and unhappy, leading a marginal existence that for some is hell on earth. As these problems are more common among the very aged, we might speculate that they will increase in future years as the proportion of the very aged increases.

One of our problems as well-meaning propagandists has been to skew the data on old age by including a lot of people who are not, in actuality, *old* in our comparisons. On the one hand, we argue that those 65 to 75, the "young old," do not really fit into the category of "aged" because they present few of the problems usually associated with old age. Then, we turn right around and lump this younger cohort into our data and use that information to argue that old age really is not so bad after all. It happens that those aged 65 to 75 represent about two-thirds of all persons 65 +. If these people are not really representative of the aged, then we have made a profound methodological error by including them in our descriptive statistics. By using the same tactic, we could paint a really positive image of late life simply by including the 55- to 64-year-olds in our data.

Some of the unhappy facts about the "old old" include:

- Almost ten percent of those aged 75 and above are institutionalized.[10] An additional 53 percent are living alone.[11]
- First admissions to mental hospitals for those 75 + are at a rate twice as high as the rate for young adults.[12]
- Depression is exceedingly common in later life, probably because of physical changes and significant losses — including loss of self-esteem.[13]
- Older white males have by far the highest suicide rate of any group in the population — over twice as high as the rate for younger males.[14]
- Almost 40 percent of all elderly have a limitation in some major activity because of a chronic health problem, and the rate of disability increases with age.[15]
- About a quarter of the aged polled by the Lou Harris organization indicated that, "This is the dreariest time of my life."[9]

Problems commonly confronted by the very aged include failing physical health, loss of strength and physical integrity, loss of status, decreasing income, widowhood, loss of self-esteem, problems with mobility, and declines in sensory acuity. So, our happy bias to the contrary, it is no wonder that many people dread getting old, and many people hate being old. Isolation, in particular, is a problem cited as being especially troublesome among the very aged; it is intertwined with both physical and emotional illness. Since it is one problem area that will yield to intervention, we will focus on isolation and its implications in the remainder of this discussion.

ILLNESS, ISOLATION, AND LONELINESS

Marjorie Fiske Lowenthal has contributed greatly to our understanding of the assumption that age-linked isolation is a correlate, and perhaps a cause, of mental illness in old age.[16] To clarify the problem, we must first realize that this concept may be a chicken-and-egg proposition; we need to ask the question of which came first, the isolation or the mental illness. In other words, is an older, isolated, mentally ill person isolated because of the anti-social behavior manifested by mental illness, or did being isolated in the first place cause or partially cause mental illness?

Lowenthal drew two samples of persons in the San Francisco Bay area to study: 534 persons aged 60 and above who were first-time admissions to mental hospitals, and 600 persons in the same age group in a stratified random sample from the community. Her objective was to determine the extent to which isolation contributed to mental illness and lower morale. Among her behavioral measures, including a morale scale, she asked the first group to list or tell her the number of their social contacts two weeks prior to the event of institutionalization; the group remaining in the community was asked to indicate the number of contacts they had had two weeks prior to being interviewed. She divided respondents into three categories: pure isolates (those with very few social contacts), semi-isolates (those with a few but essentially a very small number of social contacts, most of which were superficial), and interacters (persons with a high number of meaningful social contacts). In the hospitalized group, she was able to identify 52 pure isolates, 50 semi-isolates, and 30 interacters for study (the remaining subjects did not fall clearly into any of these categories). Lowenthal identified 30 pure isolates and 417 interacters in the community group. Three-quarters of the isolates were men, while three-quarters of the interacters were women. The isolates were four times more likely to be single than others in the population, and 79 percent were in the lowest socioeconomic group.

In order to get a clearer picture of the apparent relationship between isolation and mental illness, one would have to investigate the quality of the individual's social interactions as well as the life-long patterns of isolation and integration. This is what Lowenthal and Haven did in a 1968 follow-up study on 280 surviving subjects from the 1964 community sample. Their first observation was that social isolation seems to increase sharply at about age 75; more of the isolates in this upper age group were women who had become widowed. The investigators were able to identify four patterns of isolation among those in the sample who could now be categorized as total or semi-isolates:

Pure Isolates

- The life-long alienated; mostly single men who had never attempted to become integrated into society — 28 percent of the sample.
- The defeated; life-long marginal isolates who had tried and failed to make a place for themselves in society — 24 percent of the sample.

Semi-Isolates

- Chronic blamers, almost all of whom were single or divorced and had only casual or superficial contact with others in society — 20 percent of the sample.
- Late isolates, who made up the remainder of the group. Half of them were over age 80, the majority were women, and about two-thirds were widows who had no children.

Out of the total sample group of 280 in the 1968 follow-up, 112, or 40 percent, had some type of psychiatric disorder; 60 percent were depressed. Losses such as widowhood were clearly related to poor morale. Lowenthal and Haven conclude that life-long isolates do not have a higher rate of mental illness, whereas people who *become* isolated have much higher rates of mental illness. In other words, people who have been alone all of their lives have adapted to a solitary existence and have no particular adaptation to make in this regard to late life. Those who are used to the presence of others and interacting with them, however, have a particularly hard time accepting the loss of those contacts in old age.

Lowenthal and Haven, in their analysis of interaction, introduce another important factor, that of the *confidant*. A confidant is a person in whom one may confide, who will listen to your troubles, a close friend or relative whom you trust, who is near at hand and willing to listen to you. A man's confidant is most often his wife, if he has one. A woman's confidant would be her husband, but is as likely to be an older daughter, a sister, or a close friend. The great majority (69 percent) of the 168 psychiatrically unimpaired persons in the sample had a confidant, while only 31 percent in the impaired group had one. Again, as with interaction with others, the concept of *loss* is vital. "The great majority of those who lost a confidant are depressed, and the great majority of those who maintained one are satisfied."[17, p.102] The implication is that the presence of an intimate relationship serves as a buffer against the decrements caused by losses associated with old age.

To sum up what we can learn from these two studies, it appears that people who become isolated are quite vulnerable, while those who have always been loners will notice no appreciable change or resultant stress in this respect as they age. In other words, it is the *loss* of interaction that causes the problem. People who have at least one close, intimate relationship with another person are better off, since this confidant acts as a buffer against social loss. Those who maintain a confidant relationship are much less likely to become depressed.

In his book *The Broken Heart*, James J. Lynch analyzes census and public health data to present a persuasive case that those who are alone are much more vulnerable to physiological and mental illness.[18] Living alone, in fact, is a more important risk factor in the etiology of most causes of death than smoking, overweight, inactivity, high blood pressure, or elevated level of serum cholesterol. Among adult white males, the mortality rate for heart disease among the divorced is twice as high as the rate for those who are married; for motor vehicle accidents it is three and a half times higher; it is more than twice as high for respiratory cancer and for stroke; it is over four times higher for suicide, and seven times higher for cirrhosis of the liver.

The death rates for widowers parallel those for divorced men at a somewhat lower level for most causes of death with two important exceptions; widowed males are even more likely than the divorced to die in a vehicular accident or from suicide. Mental hospitalization rates show a similar pattern: divorced males are ten times more likely to be in a mental hospital than are married men; widowed males have a rate five times higher than those who are married. Data for females display a similar pattern. In fact, for *all* causes of death, married people have lower rates of mortality than do single, widowed, or divorced individuals. These comparisons are true for all illness-related causes of death as well as such unnatural causes as homicide, accidental falls, suicide, accidental fires or explosions, and motor vehicle accidents. Similar results to these were found in a study done by Helsing, Szklo, and Comstock, and were especially the case among widowed males.[19]

One might conclude from this information that people who live alone just don't *try* as hard to stay alive. Perhaps having a significant relationship with at least one other individual acts as a motivating factor in some way; it might simply be that these people have more to live for. Lynch concludes:

> Cancer, tuberculosis, suicide, accidents, mental disease — all are significantly influenced by human companionship. Nature uses many weapons to shorten the lives of lonely people. On a statistical basis it simply chooses heart disease most frequently.[18, p.4]

IMPLICATIONS FOR INTERVENTION:
A THEOLOGICAL CONCLUSION

Old age is no bowl of cherries. Despite the positive conclusions we might cite from the gerontological literature, a case can also be built for viewing old age for many as a time of pain and loneliness. Older adults are more vulnerable than any other age group to chronic physical and emotional illness. They are more likely to be lonely than any other age group. Isolation exacerbates many of the problems older people have, and more than half of those aged 75 and above are isolated, either living alone or in institutions. Many aged people who need services are hard to get to; some are practically invisible.

It is precisely because of these multiple problems that a ministry to the isolated elderly is such a need. Usually, we get people in our programs who are the easiest to get to — and who need the program the least. Hot lunches, bingo, and field trips are all well and good, but let's not kid ourselves as to how much real good they do. Searching out the isolated elderly and providing ministry, counseling, friendship, and building a trust relationship is a demanding and perhaps thankless task. Becoming an old man's confidant may take hours and hours of breaking down barriers and an investment of patience and understanding that many are not willing or able to make. Keeping that old man out of the mental ward is the kind of ministry that lacks in flash and style; it will not advance one's career, nor will it make one a big cheese within the denomination.

To conclude, old age does not have to be dismal; unfortunately, it is for many who have lost the ability to reach out to others. To die alone is one of our greatest terrors, one of the most basic fears that we as humans have. We are social creatures; we need one another, and solitary confinement is a torture. There are not hours in a day to visit everyone who is old and lonely, but we might spend some of our precious hours with a few. The test of a ministry with the elderly might be found in the answer to this question: "When did you visit me?"

In addition, it is wise to remember that no matter how old or miserable a person is, that, "All the truly significant emotional options remain available until the moment of death — love, hate, reconciliation, self-assertion, and self-esteem," [20, p.169] Each individual possesses worth and dignity, and every stage of life, including old age, has intrinsic value and the potential for growth and development. [21]

In summary, we see a vastly larger population of older people in the future, as well as an aging of the older population itself. While the potential for well-being is — and will be — there for most elders, late life will be equated with misery for some, just as it has always been. Current trends toward smaller families and higher rates of divorce will combine with higher numbers of people living into later life, and these trends will spell higher rates of isolation for many of the aged. We can say with some certainty that the "old old," living alone, have greater rates of depressive and other illnesses, poverty, and social isolation. Bias against the aged, as a group increasingly in need of expensive services, may also grow, while personal value and self-esteem decline. There will be a critical need for an intentional ministry to the isolated elderly.

NOTES

1. Peter Yin & Marsha Shine. Misinterpretations of increases in life expectancy in gerontology textbooks. *The Gerontologist*, 1985, *25*, 78-82.

2. Metropolitan Life Insurance Company. *Statistical Bulletin*, 1985, *66*(3).

3. James F. Fries & Lawrence M. Crapo. *Vitality and Aging*. San Francisco: Freeman, 1981.

4. Metropolitan Life Insurance Company. *Statistical Bulletin*, 1984, *65*(1).

5. James A. Thorson & Shirley A. Waskel. Future trends in education for older adults. In Ronald Sherron & D. Barry Lumsden (Eds.). *Introduction to Educational Gerontology*, Second Revised Edition. Washington, DC: Hemisphere, 1985, 223-247.

6. U.S. Bureau of the Census. *Current Population Reports*, Series p-25, No. 952, 1983.

7. David L. Klemmack, Lucinda Lee Roff, & Richard M. Durand. Who knows how much about aging? *Research on Aging*, 1980, *2*, 432-444.

8. James A. Thorson. Attitudes toward the aged as a function of race and social class. *The Gerontologist*, 1975, *15*, 343-344.

9. Lou Harris & Associates. *Aging in the Eighties: America in Transition*. Washington, DC: National Council on the Aging, 1981.

10. Erdman Palmore. Facts on aging. *The Gerontologist*, 1977, *17*, 315-320.

11. Robert C. Atchley. *Social Forces in Aging*. Belmont, California: Wadsworth, 1985.

12. Erdman Palmore. Social factors in mental illness in the aged. In Ewald Busse & Eric Pfeiffer (Eds.), *Mental Illness in Later Life*. Washington, DC: American Psychiatric Association, 1973.

13. R. Bruce Sloan. Psychiatric problems of the aged. *Continuing Education*, 1978, *9*, 42-50.

14. Robert N. Butler & Myrna I. Lewis. *Aging and Mental Health* Revised Third Edition. St. Louis: C. V. Mosby, 1982.

15. U.S. Public Health Service. *Statistical Data*, 1975.

16. Marjorie Fiske Lowenthal. Social isolation and mental illness in old age. *American Sociological Review*, 1964, *29*, 54-70.

17. Marjorie Fiske Lowenthal & Clayton Haven. Interaction and adaptation: Intimacy as a critical variable. *American Sociological Review*, 1968, *33*, 93-110.

18. James J. Lynch. *The Broken Heart*. New York: Basic Books, 1979.

19. Knud J. Helsing, Moyses Szklo, & George Comstock. Factors associated with mortality after widowhood. *American Journal of Public Health*, 1981, *71*, 802-809.

20. Myrna I. Lewis & Robert N. Butler. Life-review therapy: Putting memories to work in individual and group psycho-therapy. *Geriatrics*, 1974, *24*, 165-173.

21. Bruce J. Horacek. Life review: A pastoral counseling technique. In James A. Thorson & Thomas C. Cook. (Eds.), *Spiritual Well-Being of the Elderly*. Springfield, Illinois: Charles C Thomas, 1980, 100-107.

Theology and Aging
in the 21st Century

W. Paul Jones, PhD

SUMMARY. This article distinguishes between *diakrisis* as a futuring which extrapolates from the present to the future and *prolepsis* as an extrapolation of the present from the future. The former is critiqued as bourgeoisie projection; the latter is identified as prophetic, characteristic of a Biblical approach to reality. In Part II, nine aspects of the plight and hope for the aging are projected from a theological perspective. In Part III the theology of the 21st century is identified as destined to be written by older theologians, who, more aware of authentic living as needing to be done in the face of death, will be identifiable by twelve characteristics.

AN APPROACH TO FUTURISM

Any attempt at futuring needs to recognize two methods by which it can be done. The first is a process of interpolation from the present to the future. Such an effort attempts to project the *novum* that is latent in culture, assuming a continuity between present and future. It endeavors a realism born of documented data. The second is a process of interpolation from the future to the present, striving toward an idealism born either of belief in the power of values to change the future, or of faith in that which transcends finite reality as radical promise. Here "new" means *adventus*, the inbreaking of the unexpected and the unpredictable.[1]

While the first type of futuring tends to characterize the current

W. Paul Jones is Professor of Philosophical Theology and Director of Doctoral Studies at Saint Paul School of Theology. He has a BA in literature from Mt. Union College (1954), a BD in Bible from Yale Divinity School, a MA in Philosophy from Yale University Graduate School, and a PhD in Philosophical Theology from Yale. He has taught at Yale and Princeton Universities.

17

thinking of secular America, the second method is characteristic of the Biblical world, placing the future in paradoxical relation to the present. Yahweh was a God of the future, announcing that radically "new" things would be done—unprecedented, unpredictable, one of a kind. Relatedly, the final editors of the scripture wrote from the perspective expressed well in Psalm 137:2: "How shall we sing the Lord's song in a foreign land?" Thus it becomes evident that the Judeo-Christian world of the succeeding centuries results from an *exile* Gospel. Since in many ways ours is a post-Christian age, any futuring by a Christian theologian also will tend to be of the second type, for interpolation from the present to the future would predict continued captivity for us just as it did for Israel.

The concept of exodus illustrates well this understanding of the future standing as paradoxical fulfillment of the present hope. Exodus turned out to be not prosperity at all, but 40 years of wandering in the wilderness, and likewise, Israel's special calling turned out not to entail triumph over others but a humbling as servant suffering in behalf of all. Or again, the sought-for "King Messiah" was born in a manger, entered the capitol riding an ass, and won by losing— through his own extermination. It is not surprising, then, that whenever Christians have tried to interpolate from present to future, they have been notoriously inept, for wherever a world is made predictable and closed, it becomes for the Christian a foreign world. Rather, the Church "futures" best when it does what it has been called to be—to live "as if," vivified proleptically in the present in light of the future which comes as paradoxical promise. The Biblical illustrations are abundant. "By faith Abraham . . . went out, not knowing where he was to go. . . ." Proverbs knew that "where there is no vision, a people perish." St. Paul refused to "be conformed to this world, but be transformed. . . ." And for the writer of *Revelation*, the old has passed away, for from the perspective of the promised future we alone are able to perceive, celebrate, and give ourselves to "a new heaven and a new earth." Somehow these examples are organically related.

Theologian Letty Russell makes a similar distinction in differentiating between two types of understanding. *Diakrisis* is a process of discerning what is happening in the present so as to identify possible future outcomes. *Prolepsis*, on the other hand, is a "normative forecasting" in which one anticipates a hoped-for future in the present.

Whatever the name given, the first type of futuring is safe, only mildly imaginative, and sometimes frustratingly accurate in the short run. It inclines, however, toward the parochial, assuming that the powerful, the "controllers" of the present culture/system will remain central. Thus "secular futuring" in this country tends to be white, male, capitalistic, upper class, materialistic, western, northern, Protestant, industrial, technocratic, and above all, economic. In other words, such "futuring" operates on the assumption that significant transitions will be peaceful, controlled, and mutually beneficial, with those persons who are presently central remaining so. Even if there might occur a paradigm shift that must be recognized, it tends to be viewed so as to benefit the present power alignments.

While in the short run such projections may be accurate, futuring which, on the contrary, is on a global scale is likely to discern a contrasting outlook. For example, it is incredibly difficult to entertain that the United States, representing 7% of the world's population can in the long run continue to control 40-60% of the world's resources. For how long can the third world be expected to pay even the interest on their first world debts while increasing starvation is the result of the enlarging dynamics of austerity? And while military domination might slow the inevitabilities of such graphic inequality, the price entailed is an incredibly escalating financial debt — one can hardly grasp its magnitude. For example, it takes 30 years to count to 1 billion, yet the interest alone on our soaring national debt is 718 billion dollars each year. Therefore any careful and critical use of futuring of the first type impels one toward greater openness to futuring of the second type.

But what has this to do with aging? It means becoming aware that traditional futuring of the first type is parochial not only in being globally restricted, but even on the domestic scene the "expendables" are treated as inconsequential. And the elderly are increasingly central as "expendable." In fact, whenever the elderly do receive consideration, it is largely as a market to be captured or an electoral vote to be co-opted. While such short-run "inevitabilities" contained within the present American "system" must be taken with seriousness by the Christian theologian, at the same time these dynamics must be questioned from the perspective of value, that is, of vision. Although this second type of futuring can err by placing excess trust in the power of ideas to change reality, we cannot escape the recognition that our Christian trust is in a God who is operative *in*, *with*, and *upon* history, whose primary goal is justice. If Scripture is to be believed this Divine operation is in behalf of the maimed, the oppressed, the rejected, the powerless, and the use-less — in a word, in behalf of the "expendables."

The phenomenon of "liberation theology" is a reflection of such futuring. It includes such rhythms as "feminist theology," "Black theology," "Third World theology," "gay theology." Whatever the long-range characteristics of these developments, it needs to be written from the perspective not of the powerful but of the ones with whom the God of Jesus Christ clearly identified. There is little doubt that a "theology of aging" will be written as part of such a dynamic. In fact it is beginning to be written, with implications potentially more thoroughgoing, perhaps, than those of any of the other liberation expressions. In any case, the foreseeable future of theology would seem to rest in the work of these "expendable ones." And while the Christian must take seriously futurist Dennis Gabor's insistence upon "inventing the future," we also must ob-serve with suitable suspicion any inventions by those whose self-interest seems to be in perpetuating continuity of the unjust present with a controlled future. Moreover, on the other hand, there is a real risk in writing "liberation theology" — that of isolating theology further from those in power, for whom such theologizing needs to come as *prophetic* futuring.

Christian urbanist Kim Jefferson's critique of much of the present futuring in the United States is a helpful summary for us here. He finds it to have little vision, to be crisis-oriented, monolithic, tech-nocratic, non-global, non-integrative, non-holistic, non-prophetic about the brokenness of contemporary life, concerned for determin-ing rather than enabling a "choiceful future," and, finally, non-at-tentive to issues of racism, sexism, and elitism. By adding "age-ism" to the list, we have "completed" the large agenda for theology in the 21st century.

To turn more specifically to theological futuring regarding aging means taking a methodological approach not dissimilar to that which Letty Russell has called "adventology." This entails "the study of the future, not as it evolves from the past, but as it comes toward us from God." Here the first futurist method is taken up in service to the second. Thus *diakrisis* discerns the signs of the com-ing kingdom in the present, criticizing those factors in society which "obstruct community, peace, and justice." This method opens the way to *prolepsis* as envisagement of the future so as to render urgent the task of present change. As Russell puts it, "While future shock is maladjustment with the present because of the longed-for past, advent shock is maladjustment with the present because of the longed-for future!"[2]

AGING FROM A THEOLOGICAL PERSPECTIVE IN THE 21ST CENTURY

1. The Expendable Ones

If the projections of futurists are basically technological, eco-nomic, and monolithic, what of the elderly who by definition in our present culture are left out of the resulting scenarios? Such a question must be made part of the larger question of whether the present short-range success through military control will enable the United States in particular and capitalism in general to remain the dominant system, at least in the West. Ironically, any debilitating shifts in this current "stability" will affect first and most drastically those most vulnerable in the present "system," namely, those within the poverty sectors—primarily black, then poor white, followed by blue collar and then middle class. And within each of these sectors resides the "sub-class" of the elderly, the ones who are most vulnerable economically in each grouping.

The expendability of aging persons as it is played out in the larger world scene appears to be almost as determined as it is negative. How bleak such a future will be depends in part on the degree to which the elderly permit themselves to be caught up in the "determinism" of such a survival-preservation cycle. Alternatively, there could be a rising identification of the aging in this country with global liberation struggles, bringing a broader power base for significant systemic change. The survival cycle, however, usually creates conservatism, as the expendables frantically clutch after the little that is decreasingly left.

2. The Aged and Economic Distribution

Sociologist Haskell Miller has declared that in the United States, "a real danger exists that ownership and control will gravitate into fewer hands and that distribution will be managed for the benefit of the few rather than the welfare of all. . . ."[3] In truth, such a scenario is already operative. Over 900,000 persons entered the ranks of the official poor in 1983, an *increase* of 8.4 million in the number of poor in this country from 1979 to 1983. The poor now constitute 35.3% of our population, with the proportion of elderly poor being higher than any other age group. At the same time, in 1982 the richest 20% of Americans received more income than the bottom 70% combined, the differential moving to an all time discrepancy. It is no wonder that Charles Krauthammer, Senior Editor of *The New Republic*, has concluded that, "Capitalism in its pure form is Darwinian." In decided contrast to such tendencies stands the declaration of the recent "Pastoral Letter on Social Teachings and the U.S. Economy" by the National Conference of Catholic Bishops. In reaction to the plight of the expendables, the task of the Christian is characterized this way: "to ensure that no one among us is hungry, homeless, unemployed, or otherwise is denied what is necessary to live with dignity." There is identified here a clear preferential commitment to the poor in general and to the aged as one of the focused particulars. Consequently, the crucial struggle for the next generation will center on whether or not adjustments in the present economic system of this country will be sufficient. The Catholic Bishops believe so, holding that this "government has a positive moral function: that of protecting basic rights, ensuring economic justice for all and enabling citizens to coordinate their actions toward these ends." This as the clear commitment to which Christians are called is hardly debatable; but as a goal that is intrinsic to our present economic system, it is hardly entertainable. The Social Security system is a case in point. There seems to be little governmental commitment to the elderly unless the system itself is economically self-sustaining. Predictably, recent poles indicate that the majority of working persons do not trust that they will ever profit from the Social Security system when they retire, even though they have paid into it throughout their working life. All of this stands in graphic contrast to a proposed space-based defense system that former Secretary of Defense James Schlesinger projects will cost $1 trillion. Even without it, by 1990 military spending will cost $34,000 yearly for a family of four. The United Methodist Council of Bishops anticipates this consequence: "The human costs of the buildup in the name of 'defense' are born most directly by those who are actually most defenseless: the poor, the elderly, and the very young."[4]

In many ways the present conflict between this country and some of those labeled "Communist" (e.g. Cuba), hinges on an alternative system that at least in goal is different from our present economic system as it is compatible with the Biblical vision. The Christian

commitment is to guaranteed access for all persons to whatever is
needed for the wholeness of life, simply because one exists. It is a
guarantee that every aged person will have free shelter, food, medical and hospital care, continuing education, recreation, etc. sufficient for the completion of life. These are the same benefits belonging to every worker, with "profit" becoming a consideration only
after these fundamental needs are met. The contrast between the
Cuban system and the growing "sectors of expendability" occurring in the United States situation must lead to a serious consider
ation, at least for Christians, of a new visioning of alternative systemic expressions. Such a vision is presently energizing the "rising" nations; the future depends in part on the degree to which the
expendables in this country, especially the growing number of aged,
are able to envisage such a common cause.

3. World Tensions and the Age Polarity

The present politico-military alignments are predicated on the assumption that the two super-powers must polarize the global dynamic into a life-and-death struggle between West and East. Increasing evidence, however, indicates that the real struggle as we
approach the 21st century is between North and South. Much of the
development of "Western civilization" has been at the expense of
the exploitation of non-European peoples, peoples of the "South."
Their increasing rebellion threatens to entail Western and Eastern
banking crises, loss of neo-colonial markets, and non-control of
increasingly scarce raw materials, suggesting that the future resides
in the hands of these oppressed. In fact the present East-West relation is, ironically, an unrecognized hegemony, at present teetering
on a tenuous imperialism on both sides.
Regardless of the economic effects of this dynamic upon the expendables in the West, however, an even more crucial dynamic will
be at work: at the same time that the median age in the U.S. steadily
rises to a record high, the median age of the third world is 12 years!
This makes the differential two-and-one-half-times higher in this
country. By the year 2000 one-half of Latin America's population
will be under 21 years of age. When we focus on the alienation in
this country between post-retirement adults and "youth," we dimly
begin to realize how this dynamic is destined to become a primary
global dynamic. That is, unless our present style of socializing
across age groups is changed, the future is destined to be difficult

indeed. In a recent visit to Nicaragua, I probably reflected many in this country in finding it difficult at first to take seriously the youthful leaders occupying even the highest posts; they in turn, it would seem, are becoming increasingly disenchanted with the socialization they have received to respect elders, at least as these elders tend to represent the power nations. It is of no minor significance that the elected president of Nicaragua is one of the youngest in present governments, while the president of the United States is the oldest in our country's history. It may well be that the confounding corollary of the widening global polarity of haves and have-nots will be a global generation gap. Age is destined to be an increasingly central but as yet unrecognized factor on the global scene.

4. Vocation as Pilgrimage

Although there is an increase in the number of factors encouraging both greater automation and a decline in labor needs, the movement toward expendability through unemployment could be revised (even reversed), if pressure for doing so were to be mobilized. For example, by redistributing labor needs across the entire population, a new norm of early retirement could expand the whole idea of "second career," now limited to retirees from the military. But since the opportunity for second career employment will be ever more unlikely, we might begin to envisage, instead, something similar to a "multi-vocational development" characteristic of Confucian society. Within that culture, independent of economic reward, was a clear awareness that the broad aging process brought different abilities, sensitivities, needs, and interests. Analogously, our present society is undergoing thorough social reexamination of the once widely-held assumption making normative a life-time commitment of each person to one other person; thus we can begin to doubt that one "vocational" calling per lifetime is adequate fulfillment for being human. It is interesting here to hear the Trappist monk Matthew Kelty as he discussed the vocation of being a monk. It should never be entered, he said, until one's moral life is pretty well in hand. "Monks are sinners," he confessed, "but they all feel too that a man should finish his soup before he goes on to the next course."[5] In other words, what is "right" for a person in the twenties is hardly fulfilling in mid-life, as suggested by the crisis that many experience at that point. Nor is personal advancement in a continuous life line apt to provide the needed stages of growth. Instead, current research is indicating that life has stages, each with its "fitting-ness." The period that we now call "aged" can be redefined not as retirement (i.e., from meaningful action) but as transition into yet a different stage of existing. Many cultures see the "aged" as special, uniquely able to bring a tranquil attitude to life as a whole, whereby to tell stories that distill meaning, contemplate life's inner meanings, and face with courage life's outer boundaries — in a word, to seek wisdom by being wise. In this country, however, the normative stages defining life are pre-employment, employment, and post-employment. Perhaps, surprisingly, it is the innocuous nature of the present post-employment stage that can bring prophetic judgement on all three stages, and in so doing, call for a value reorientation more fitting to the stages characteristic of individual growth into wholeness.

Moreover, wisdom has, in most cultures, been connected with spirituality. Thus the expendability of the aged in this country may well be associated with the marginalizing of religion, thereby squandering the contribution which makes the aged unique and inexpendable. This may account for why the majority of churches have a heavily-elderly membership. Yet contemporary Christianity has not sensed that the elderly have a unique calling, holding instead that an aging church indicates a fatal situation, measuring significance in terms of youth. Were we to perceive the predominant presence of the elderly as calling, it is conceivable that the church may become aware of its rare prophetic possibilities for social spiritual renewal, insisting upon a holistic pilgrimage for each human as the norm.

5. The Aged as Electoral Factor

Many times society lumps individuals into groupings that have no political or power significance, e.g. left-handed persons. Similarly, until recently, gay individuals represented such a wide spectrum of opinions on most subjects that they were not politically differentiable from the general population. This is no longer true. Correlatively, a crucial issue for the aged in the coming years will be the degree to which their increasing marginalization, in tension with their growing numbers, will enable sufficient commonality of interests for them to become a significant electoral power. That is, while the primary spectrum today among the elderly is becoming economic, a bleak economic future could well mark a significant narrowing of the distractions of this spectrum, bringing self-interest to an organizable momentum. To be deprived of what one once had is a far more powerful impetus than to demand what one never had. The issue will be whether growing deprivation leads to a survival stance of conservative defensiveness or brings demands for significant systemic alteration. It is becoming clearer that the aging sector, while presently one of the most unorganized, is potentially the most available (certainly regarding time) for political action. In addition, it is one of the most visible of the expendables as a potential swing vote.

6. Compartmentalization and Holism

The aged are experiencing an increasing compartmentalization, especially as economic factors identify this sector of the population for specialized marketing. The resulting "ghettoization" of the elderly is evidenced in housing, in geography, in total care communities, in nursing homes. Such a process leads inevitably to socializing elders into a marketable "sub-class" of people who are not so much responded to as they are formed by being told what their pre-set expected behavior is to be — at best a paternalism by stereotyping. "Elderly people do this, want that, like their own company, seek leisure, etc." This dynamic is so operative today that we are hard-pressed to differentiate between cause and effect. A key factor for the 21st century will be the inner effect such compartmentalization will have on the quality of life experienced. The increasing and disproportionately high number of attempts at suicide by elders bespeak the emptiness, the trappedness, and/or the corrosive boredom endemic to this compartmentalized lifestyle. Such silent pleas for holism can make common cause throughout the present population, running the gamut from the loss of holism symbolized by the family farm, through the forfeiture of the extended family for the isolated nuclear family, to the "burnout" increasingly characteristic of corporate commitment. The future depends on the degree to which this underbelly of the "unused self" suffers in silent isolation or becomes a groundswell of restless discontent. For the Christian it is clear that just as "bread" for the elderly is mandatory, not to live by bread alone is equally normative. But if employment has been socialized in the larger society as synonymous with meaning, what is left for the elderly? Etymologically, to "retire" means "to draw back." If left there, it marks the entry into programmed entropy.

Whatever may come of this, there is little doubt that the next generation will be marked by much inner suffering, resulting either in a holocaust of the spirit or a potentially powerful force for change.

7. The New Leisure

The ever-growing expendableness of labor through determined automation of the workforce will be coupled with the cost of training specialists who meet the demands for increasingly technical employment. These specialists will create pressure for giving more employment hours for fewer people, with late-retirement an option for the few, early-retirement the increasing norm for the many. Since part-time employment after retirement will become less available, a greater number of persons will be forced to explore genuine lifestyles that are at odds with the present norm. This might lead, on the one hand, to radical demands for ascetic and simple life styles no longer determined by ownership, competition, consumption, laborsaving gadgetry—in effect, by middle class comfort. On the other hand, the entry of younger "retirees" into the present ethos of retirement villages will mark such living as genuinely unappealing to middle-aged energies, needs, and interests. Such interaction may add to the pressure for alternative value-formation. Can it be that boredom and decreasing income possibilities can converge as a powerful impetus for change in the recognizable future?

8. Spiritualization and the Aging Process

In the history of Christian theology a decisive wedge has pervasively divided a "theology of doing" from a "theology of being." We have experienced the former in this country primarily in the expression called the "Protestant work ethic." Here the justification that gives identity and thus meaning to life centers in work, activity, production, performance, capability, achievement—with the dynamic of performance-reward being equivalent in human behavior to that of cause and effect in the physical domain. "Great shall be your reward" sets the tone both for this life and for the one to come. A "theology of being," on the other hand, centers in grace, not as the consequence of human action but as the free and liberating premise for genuine living, from which meaningful action follows spontaneously rather than as requirement. As a professor of theology I continue to marvel at how difficult it is for ministerial students socialized in this country to grasp the idea of grace. Grace means that the sacredness of life rests in the graciousness of a God who loves even the sparrows with infinite and tender love, no matter what the condition or quality or the lack of "goodness" of the one loved. This "good news" is mind boggling for those of us who were raised to believe that only the deserving should receive, and that such reception should be in direct proportion to ability and circumstance of activity. And so it would seem that as the number of elderly in this country steadily increases, a "theological" crisis is in the making.

The crisis begins as an empty worthlessness erupting shortly after retirement. Suddenly one no longer "does" for a living, but is destined from now on simply "to be." Without preparation, without even an understanding of such a state, the "conversion" is a nightmare rather than entry into abundant life. It may turn out that such a crisis will be a new wilderness for the receptivity of a way of existence beginning to be identified today as "spiritual." Elsewhere I have explored this "spirituality of being," which seems to be arising especially among the aging, as it correlates with the primary dimensions of the aging process itself.[6] Such spirituality provides common ground between Roman Catholics and the followers of Luther. Reminiscent of the Reformers we hear the words of Thomas Merton: "God loves us irrespective of our merits and whatever is good in us comes from His life, not from our own doing." In fact, the role Merton sees for the monk may well be the prophetic role awaiting the elderly as calling: "It is the peculiar office of the monk in the modern world to keep the way open for modern technological man [sic] to recover the integrity of his own inner depths."[7] Likewise the feminist insistence upon humans as gentle guests in creation can hear as cohort the patient participation that becomes increasingly possible for the elder.

9. Creative Models for an Experimental Future

It is time for the Church to recognize the tainted love it has exercised so often toward the elderly, acknowledging that what has been done caters principally to the affluent, offering for sale the luxuries of retirement living. The call in the next decade and beyond is to venture creative experiments that do not compete with or duplicate available services. There is a heavy need for signal models of holism that will serve as genuine alternatives to an ethos in which the elderly are marginal, expendable, tolerated, and, at best, served. Needed is not the Church's ministry *to* the aged but rather a context *for* aged ministry to the society. The possibilities contained in some of the experimental "Zionic communities" related to the R.L.D.S. church are impressive. If Zion is to be the goal promised for creation, we need experiments as proleptic leaven in the present. Here may be attempted: intergenerational communities; block employment scheduling, necessitating shorter work periods by linking persons chronologically in cooperative employment; labor intensive restoration of lost skills and products of rare beauty; music created for its own sake; non-traditional intimacies; preventative and holistic health environments; cooperative ownership and use; multiple education for the love of learning; fulfillment in each person of once aborted "vocational dreams."

In his final lecture Merton mused that if the Marxist dream (from each according to one's abilities, to each according to one's needs) were a possibility, it would be in a monastery. The early church likewise regarded this as a possibility for the serious Christian community, for each brought "the money received" and "the money was distributed to each one according to his [sic] need" (Acts 4:34-35). However we might conclude the issue, Marx's vision of a typical day in the "classless society" is intriguing. It is one in which each day is new, in which we choose each morning whether to go fishing, to be an administrator, to write music, or to try our hand at poetry. Such "romanticism" was a vision sufficient for him to advocate revolution. To paraphrase Merton, if such a vision is possible it most likely will be in a Christian community of elders, creating the good for all by the pooling of labor, benefits, opportunities, where above all the body of Christ recognizes as necessary every type and every fibre, where no longer can one doubt that in the end none shall pass unwanted. Such models for the 21st century are deeply needed, by those willing to risk failure. Perhaps only the church can rediscover such motivation and risk such "dreams." Otherwise the future is likely to be bleak: By her own account in the book *Disguised: A True Story*, 33-year-old Patricia Moore emerged from a three-year disguise as an 85-year-old person "physically scarred, emotionally battered, [and] incredulous at the way she was treated."[9]

AGING AND THE THEOLOGY
OF THE 21ST CENTURY

Elsewhere I have developed a case for "Gerontheology." [10] It rests on the assumption shared by thinkers as diverse as Augustine and Heidegger that the meaning of life is determined by how we die our death. Consequently, the aging process potentially is a powerful theologizing adventure. Yet death for our present culture is perhaps the most hidden and avoided phenomenon. [11] And so this stance of avoidance is an important factor in accounting for the anti-theological posture of many persons today. As I have expressed elsewhere, [12] ageism may well be the outcome precisely of this current effort to avoid death by rendering invisible the elderly as symbolic harbingers of our final expendability. If religion is, as a matter of fact, one's posture shaped in relationship to death's inevitability, the active presence of the self-aware elderly provides an important factor in the emergence of a theology of the next decade and beyond. Put another way, the aged appear as a major conundrum for the coming century because death is the final barrier proposing the parameters marking mystery. Merton wisely observes that Christianity necessarily calls us into the wilderness. "The convocation of Israel in the wilderness of Sinai is the story of God leading men [sic] on what appears to be a 'march into the open gates of death' (Mauser)." [13] If the monastic calling is to preserve the wilderness against every modern effort at domestication, then the elder (facing with daily self-consciousness the inevitable limits less visibly facing all of us) is the religious subversive in the belly of that society. I remember vividly the outlook of Harvard theologian Arthur McGill after a serious sickness that was eventually to take his life. "When one stares death helplessly in the face," he said, "without any possibility of hiding, it renders insignificant much of what one once pursued with absolute passion." For him such a "final" posture was what it meant to theologize "from under the cross." "Otherwise," he claimed, "the good news of resurrection is romantic escape." Perhaps no single statistic will be more important in shaping the theology of the future than this one: in 1900 one half of all deaths were among children; in 1980, two thirds of all deaths were among persons over 65, with children accounting for only 6%. Increasingly, death is being reserved for an ever-growing aging population.

Futurist Larry A. Jackson discerns the faith of the church of the future in a similar way: the central faith will be that "the ultimate ground of our being and of creation is, finally, a mystery." [14] It is difficult to "prophesy" more, except to observe that the professional theologians in this country will have a mean age higher than ever before, bringing with it a consequent shift in perspective. In addition, if theological "answers" correlate with existential questions, as Paul Tillich claimed, one might hunch that theology written from an "aging perspective" would emphasize the following characteristics: a Christology of incarnation (Emmanuel "God with us"); God under the image of confidant, with a heavy emphasis upon immanence experienced sacramentally in commonday objects and experience; faith centering in grace; a spirituality of interior presence; death as transition into Mystery; Christian life as constituted by recognizably unique and equally valid "stages along life's way"; liturgy as celebration of life's rhythms, finding analogies emerging from nature rather than from history; sacraments as hinge events marking life as pilgrimage; ecclesiology stressing the Body of Christ as organic community incorporating a rich multiplicity of persons and lifestyles; an ethic where love becomes more promissorial and less experiential; a social ethic characterized by ecological organism; and life as the entry and exit of one invited as gentle guest to nurture the creation into being, much as a mother rocks a manger/crib, or a poet giggles an ecstatic spring into being, or a craftsperson's finger sands into final perfection a carving of ancient oak.

NOTES

1. See Braaten, Carl. *Christ and Counter Christ* (Philadelphia: Fortress, 1972), pp. 2-23.

2. Russell, Letty. "The Role of the Church in the City: Anticipation of the Promise." In *From Vision to Strategies: A Workbook for Urban Ministries*, United Methodist Office of Urban Ministries.

3. Miller, Haskell. "Making Our Dollars Count for Human Need," *Circuit Rider*, July/August 1985, p. 8.

4. "In Defense of Creation: The Nuclear Crisis and a Just Peace." A statement being prepared by the United Methodist Council of Bishops, January 1986, p. 44.

5. Kelty, Matthew, O.C.S.O., *Aspects of the Monastic Calling*, Abbey of Gethsemani, Trappist, Kentucky, p. 38.

6. Jones, W. Paul. "Aging as a Spiritualizing Process," *Journal of Religion and Aging*, vol. 1, no. 1, 1984, pp. 3-16.

7. Merton, Thomas. *The Monastic Journey* (Garden City: Doubleday, 1978), p. 221.

8. *Ibid.*, p. 13.

9. *Lawrence Journal-World*, Lawrence, Kansas, February 11, 1986, p. 6.

10. Jones, W. Paul. "Geronthcology: Spirituality and Aging." In *Quarterly Papers on Religion and Aging*, Oubri A. Popple Center for Health and Welfare Studies, vol. 1, no. 1, Summer 1984.

11. Stannard, David E. *The Puritan Way of Death* (New York: Oxford University Press, 1977), esp. Chapter 7.

12. Jones, W. Paul. "Death as a Factor in Understanding Modern Attitudes Toward the Aging: A Symbolization-Avoidance Theory," this volume.

13. Merton, *Monastic Journey*, p. 190.

14. Jackson, Larry A. "Keeping the Faith," *The Futurist*, October 1985, pp. 26-28.

Coming Issues
in the Pastoral Care
of the Aged

Robert E. Buxbaum, DMin, CSW-ACP

SUMMARY. In the context of a growing aging population, this paper begins with the notion that the traditional resources of pastoral care will remain relevant, effective and basic. However, the Church must redefine its images of "successful" ministry to emphasize the inherent value of the gray church. Gerontological studies need to become integrated in the whole enterprise of theological education and should be recognized as both presenting a special opportunity for female clergy and for developing a new model of ministry. Discussed are three needs for adequate preparation for the pastoral care of the aged: (1) Training in group process, (2) Skills in conflict resolution, and (3) A theology of aging that rests on Grace rather than works and that separates aging as a process distinct from death and dying. Finally, the author insists upon the involvement of the aged as a prerequisite for authenticity in each of these areas.

PROLOGUE

The invitation to reflect upon the pastoral care issues in ministry to the aging at the coming turn of the century has made me profoundly aware of how much a man of the past and present I have become over the years. I remember a time when my life was principally focused on the anticipation of the future; as though completion

---

The Rev. Robert E. Buxbaum is a Presbyterian clergyman and clinical social worker who practices psychotherapy, marriage, family and group counseling with Robert E. Buxbaum and Associates, 9143 Welles Way, San Antonio, Texas 78240. A Lecturer in Pastoral Care at the Oblate School of Theology and an Adjunct Faculty in the Doctor of Ministry Program at McCormick Theological Seminary, he maintains an active ecumenical involvement in the preparation of clergy for ministry.

33

of the next achievement would be the signal that life could begin. Even though I have devoted a majority of my professional career to the practice of interpersonally oriented psychotherapy, rummaging around in my own and other peoples' pasts for meanings that help understand and facilitate the living of the present, much of my work and orientation has been implicitly directed toward the successful achievement of desired goals and an improved quality of life for the future. When I was thirty-five, I probably could have written this paper easily; confident in my ability to predict and even be definitive about my goals for decades hence. In my early fifties, having come through the mid-life transitions, I discover that I'm far more hesitant to predict the future, reluctant to put the focus of life at some point in the future and modestly guarded about the degree to which the human aspects of life really change anyway. Part of this may be explained by my being middle aged. The most significant goals held a decade or two ago have been attained. I find myself more interested in preserving the past than I would have thought possible and more uncertain about where a meaningful future lies than is comfortable. Of course, living in the here and now is one of the characteristics of the aging and I suspect that it may simply mean that I am in the normal process of my own aging!

Living in the here and now seems predicated on several tasks. First, we must come to terms with the past. It is not enough to simply acquire an intellectualized comprehension of one's history. It is also required that the past be owned, felt, grieved for and forgiven; emotionally releasing the weight it has imposed upon us and freeing the creative potential which is often its unsuspected legacy. Second, living in the here and now requires that we have a relative level of satisfaction with the present. When the degree of dissatisfaction with the present is too painful, we'd have to be crazy *not* to live in the past, in a fantasy or in a psychosis. But one of the end products of owning and forgiving the past is that we may come to see how the past has brought us to where we are now with a profound sense of blessing for whatever is experienced as genuinely "good" in the today of our lives. This doesn't imply that there are no current dissatisfactions; only that for most of us our personal history has brought us to the very best today that it is possible for us to have. Finally, those who live in the here and now increasingly bless this day as the legitimate arena where life is experienced rather than as a bridge to another day when we shall begin to live. At my age, it only fleetingly occurs to me that it is always possible that there might not be another day for me . . . and so the profound sense that many older people have that the experience of waking up in the morning is a gift has not yet permeated my awareness. My recollection of one of my father's favorite sayings ("After 50 you're on borrowed time") leads me to believe that I can anticipate that the value of each day will become increasingly conscious.

A NEW APPROACH TO PASTORAL CARE?

My grounding in the past and present seems also to have its roots in my religious life. I've always been more curious (read: anxious?) about dying than about life after death. My immersion in the part of the Christian tradition that takes its identity from looking back to the history of the people of God and historically identifiable saving event that happened in the past and may reoccur in the present, has contributed to focusing me in the past and present rather than the future. This same sense of tradition informs my approach to pastoral care so deeply that when the day comes that pastors make their calls in space ships I cannot but believe that they will bring the same essential traditional resources that have been the catalytic symbols among people and between humanity and God that have been part of our pastoral armamentarium since the Upper Room and before. Notions about appropriate leadership style have changed several times in the twenty-five years since my own ordination and may be expected to continue to change. But human nature does not change. And the need for reconciliation through incarnational representation of Word and Sacrament remains. Therefore, I anticipate no new technology of ministry. Rather it is hoped that we may anticipate a level of pastoral care that is increasingly authentic and insightful rather than different. Symbolic of this movement toward commitment to incarnational presence in pastoral care is the growing acceptance of personal psychotherapy for clergy and the expansion of gerontological studies; both of which should move us in this direction.

From the perspective that the traditional pastoral resources are an inherently viable expression of God's response to human needs, they will be as important for the future as they have been in the past. I do not look for significant changes in the essential pastoral functions in the care of the aged at the year 2000 or even beyond. But, other kinds of changes will most certainly occur. Since the demographics indicate that there will be so many more people over 50 or 65 by the century's end, there will be much more opportunity and need for ministry with a sensitivity to the realities of aging than ever before. There will be a substantial quantitative increase in need for specialized pastoral services even if the approaches to pastoral care remain essentially similar. Perhaps this distinction needs more clarification. As I would understand it, the essence of pastoral care is in the re-presentation of The Good News of God's forgiving and healing love through incarnational presence, the sharing of The Word, the administration of the Sacraments and the embrace of the sharing community of God's people in the midst of the struggles of life. Everything else in pastoral care is program; important only as it contributes to the essential. When the geriatric population increases, the need becomes numerically larger but the essential response remains the same. While not denying that each age group has its distinctive characteristics (thereby giving unique expression to its needs), we nevertheless maintain that through all time and at all ages within any epoch of history, we are much more alike than different.

HOW SHALL WE MEET THIS NEED?

It is reported that in the mainline Protestant denominations there are an increasing number of people who are seeking entrance into the Church's full-time professional ministry. We occasionally hear of having more ordained clergy than are needed and some people worry about personnel placement. In my own denomination clergy are heard to speak anxiously about how much more difficult it is to "move" than it once was and sorry indeed is the church whose Pastoral Nominating Committee does not receive several scores of dossiers of prospective candidates. To the extent that our seminaries have overlooked the demographic realities and the specific needs of the aging, the opportunity for effective future placement of personnel goes largely unrecognized. Specializations in gerontology within the ministry are the wave of the future to at least the degree to which specializations in Christian Education were in the 1940's and 1950's! But even more basic is the currently unmet need to re-orient our efforts at training pastors to recognize the needs and opportunities presented by the graying of the Church so that their pastoral care may be both appropriate and rewarding.

To be appropriate, young men and women are going to need help in walking into the world of the older person. It is not easy for the young (except the *very* young) to appreciate the dimensions of the world of the aged. Ultimately such learning demands that the ego's insistence upon proving competence be set aside long enough to learn from the aged. They alone can teach the young pastor about the emotional, physical, social and spiritual realities of the aged. Appropriateness depends upon this kind of existential involvement with those who are there.

To be rewarding, success in parish ministry needs to be redefined from having lots of young families in attendance to the provision of an opportunity to have meaningful relationships in God's community of the faithful. How many times I have heard people (including the propagandized elderly themselves) say: "We have to get young people into this church. They will be the leaders of tomorrow." I always want to ask: "Why? When the current older members die, won't there be anyone left who is then old?" Philosophy and religion have always been high among the interests of the aged. It has traditionally been the elders to whom respect and trust have been given in the Church. And yet it is common to hear people within the Church unconsciously give expression to the prejudices of ageism. It is well known that the aged all too often accept the stereotypes about themselves as if they must be true. It is a pastoral function to challenge stereotypes of all kinds; including this one! When youth is seen as the hope of the future, then it humanly follows that "success" will be measured by what success one has in ensnaring the young. A pastor of my acquaintance moved into leadership in a flourishing parish of largely middle age and older adults. The content of the program and the particular emphasis of the ministry had met their own perceived needs. Within a short time, his drive to "get young families" and involve children at the expense of the cherished aesthetics of music and worship had so changed the life of that parish that it no longer met the needs of many of its older members. His stereotype of the flourishing, successful church was so strong that he was unable to see that he already had one! His insensitivity to the quality of life issues that are often typical of the older segment of our population led to alienation, angry departures of members and a personal sense of bewildering frustration for the pastor.

The second dimension of the Church's personnel problem is the adequate utilization of the competencies of female clergy. The difference between justice and injustice, ideal and reality, remains and the result is that in my own denomination, which has been ordaining women for more than twenty-five years, female clergy still seldom occupy positions of senior pastor in our more viable congregations. In specialized ministries and denominational work the picture is not quite so bleak. The potential for women to have a major role in ministry to the aged should not be overlooked as a uniquely meaningful ministry to which female clergy bring some special qualifications. Since the older person has frequently integrated the male/female characteristics within their own emotional life and interests, they are more open to ministry without concern for the sexual identity of the ministering person. Historically, the care of the aged has most often been best provided by females whose roles had traditionally included both nurturing and catalytic functions. Finally, since the aged will become such a large segment of our church membership, those who minister to them will find themselves in increasingly influential roles.

The magnitude of the job ahead, and the availability of professionally trained clergy, present us with a unique opportunity to reconsider Protestantism's long-standing model of ministry that is primarily individualistic in design. Most Protestant clergy are trained to be an ecclesiastical Lone Ranger. Little or no attention is paid to the possibility of designing models for ministry that are truly shared efforts. "Team Ministry" has often been a misnomer for the loose coordination of several people doing distinctive, often "specialized" tasks rather than a genuine sharing of ministry. Perhaps we can do better than have a new breed of isolates; professionally trained specialists in gerontology! Perhaps we can restyle the pastoral ministry with a flexibility and integrity that is not divided by predetermined function but united by opportunity and need. Perhaps a model in which role is defined by need and opportunity rather than by seniority or stereotypical grouping is within the realm of possibility. We would need to develop radically new approaches to training clergy in which we learn to approach problems and opportunities by group processes rather than by authority or jurisdiction. One implication of this is that gerontological studies would need to be integrated into the Master of Divinity curriculum not as a speciality, but as the culminating life stage that either integrates the human enterprise or collapses into the despair of isolation and alienation. The seminary graduate that is untrained in, or insensitive to, gerontological experience is unprepared for pastoral ministry to people of *any* age. The tasks of the final stage of life may provide the long missing unitive theme for theological education as the reference for biblical, historical, ethical and pastoral studies. After all, the evaluation of the life that has been lived is where all of life experience is moving. To be able to look back upon that life and feel contented that our creation was good is the stewardship accounting we offer to God.

NEEDED: TRAINING IN GROUP PROCESS

Those who would minister to the aged will need to master the skills of group process and leadership. The sheer numbers to be ministered to will make the traditional one-to-one approach of pastoral care both inefficient and impractical. But, even more important, the basic concerns of older people frequently make the group setting the methodology of choice for pastoral care. The opportunity to hear others speak of their feelings about their problems in living, and search for ways to resolve or accept those feelings, is helpful to many people in and of itself. In group work, participants receive permission from each other to talk about the feelings that trouble them most but which they have kept hidden in the conviction that they were unacceptable, shameful and/or unique. Hidden feelings corrode the spirit and cannot be healed. Feelings thought to be unacceptable induce guilt. Shame breeds loneliness and the demon of uniqueness condemns to anxious solitude. Whereas, shared feelings find the beginning of healing in the sharing process.

The group setting begins to address the needs of the older person for meaningful friendships, the mutual trust of genuine community and intimacy. In discussing individual but often common problems together, group members build emotional attachments, and each experience of having been heard and understood establishes ties. Trust builds. The group becomes the surrogate family in which one learns to speak openly of significant things and to hear others' struggles for openness with patience and empathy. The process provides opportunities to minister to each other through the movement toward openness that establishes caring presence. "I can share my feelings and help others share theirs; for a moment I'm important to someone." This ministry is incarnational in the best sense of that word. It is clear to all that none can "do" anything about each others' problems except to "be with" one another in the gifts of attentiveness, mutual compassion and identification. This ministry to one another is, in turn, an antidote to the erosion of self-esteem that comes with the increasing feelings of helplessness and uselessness that have accompanied the aging process. Even though the content of the life experiences under discussion may be painful and negative, the process of having ministered to each other re-infuses life with opportunities to be both helpful and useful to others. The overall experience is upbeat because of the rewards intrinsic to the peer support of group process. Self-esteem is enhanced. And, since group members are frequently at different stages in coping with different problems, they offer each other a hopeful model that the sharing process can be trusted to work! "I remember when I felt that way," they reassure each other with compassion rather than arrogance. The implication is that since I no longer feel exactly that way, something that goes on here among us may be helpful in changing that for you too. They have not aged beyond the possibility of helping each other.

As a discipline, pastoral care has retained its historical preoccupation with individual relationships as the arena for most pastoral work. The ease with which pastoral counseling imitated the privacy of the physician's consulting room grew partially out of our own tradition of the privacy of the confessional, our notions about pastoral confidences and even our theological ideas about individual salvation. Further endorsed by 19th century Victorian assumptions about privacy and modesty, few clergy trust group process or believe that others do. We overlook the degree to which our society has become open in its discussion of the most intimate areas of life that would have been believed to be impossible of group disclosure even a few decades ago. Although some people need and benefit from the private setting in order to learn to begin to trust that others can respond without shock or judgement, few cannot benefit by moving on into group settings. Yet, apart from some attention paid the leadership of congregational worship, I am unaware of any seminary in the United States that makes any concerted effort to help its students learn the pastoral care functions of group construction, function, process or leadership. Few clergy have been part of the learning that can only occur when they have experienced the power of being a part of an intimate sharing group and fewer still have much clarity about how they would lead such a group. The net result is that few groups that provide the kind of opportunity for ministry to older persons exist in our churches and that this important modality for the pastoral care of the aged is far too frequently lost. Supervised experience in group process and leadership must be wedded to both gerontology and pastoral studies.

NEEDED: SKILLS IN CONFLICT RESOLUTION

The growing number of older persons may be expected to increase the level of intergenerational conflict. One pastor of a Florida church in a retirement community has described the conflict that arises around such common events as the slow older driver and the shopper for whom the trip to the store is the outing for the day and their younger neighbors who are used to moving more rapidly to meet busy schedules. Both of the older neighbors are obstacles in their way; often the recipients of anger born of frustration. Even more serious conflict can be anticipated around the economic issues of the growing cost of the maintenance and care of the aged. As the population bulge moves into the retirement years, the cost of the social security system and other care giving systems will be borne by a smaller percentage of the population; resulting in higher per person costs to each younger taxpayer. They can be expected to resent the growing burden and their reaction to these greater demands upon their limited resources may find expression in anger. And as more people live longer, the middle years of life, which have been fantasized as the time to enjoy freedom beyond the responsibility of parenting children, are becoming transformed into years of trading the earlier responsibility for children for years of being equally responsible for aging parents. The number of people well into their sixties who have continuing responsibility for the care of parents in their late eighties and early nineties is increasing. This responsibility is often experienced as a burden and is sometimes endured only because the alternative seems to be the guilt that would come from abandonment.

In a time when frequent geographical relocation has become the norm for the American family, many of the problems attendant to the individuation process of early adulthood have been avoided rather than resolved. Distance fools us into believing that they no longer exist; having somehow evaporated in the years that have intervened since leaving home. Then the day comes that they reappear and everyone is caught by surprise. Adult children are dismayed by the emotional power of their own responses. Aged parents are shocked by the appearance of hostility whose causes seem anything but evident. The needs of aged parents reawaken resentments that have smoldered unnoticed since those same kinds of needs went unmet when they parented their now adult children. It becomes apparent that the adult child's fantasy that someday they would be parented in the way they had needed or wanted disappears as parental limitations, frailties and dependency become undeniable. And even if the adult child becomes acclimated to the notion that the early life deprivation will always remain unfulfilled, they may resent that their first opportunity to take care of themselves is interrupted by the needs of their parents. And even in the best of emotionally mature parent-adult child relationships, earlier unresolved unconscious conflicts will be exacerbated by the tensions generated by role exchange and redefinition.

The pastoral roles of being an advocate for loving and significant interpersonal relationships and a facilitator of reconciliation among the alienated make conflict resolution one of the important skills employed in pastoral care. But conflict resolution is preceded by the surfacing and definition of conflicting issues and feelings; a process often uncomfortable for the pastor. Conflict and peacemaking are generally understood as antithetical rather than sequential and the pastor and people may experience the invitation to open conflict as role dystonic. Since approval needs tend to be high among clergy, behavior that invites anger may also be ego dystonic. Combined with whatever conflicts are unsettled in their relationships with their own parents, pastors may find this dimension of their pastoral care particularly difficult and/or distasteful.

It is sometimes rationalized that it is more comfortable and kinder to deny, mask or suppress anger than to deal with it openly. We have all heard it said that an adult child would confront their parent about some important issue *if* it just weren't that they were too old to understand, to change or to make a significant enough difference. Others would like to believe that God and/or the pastor will be able to make things "right" without the tumult and pain of the laceration that is the prelude to healing.

To the degree that the pastor is comfortable in accepting the expression of anger and conflict as a healthy part of normal interpersonal relationships, to the extent that she/he would rather talk about emotional realities than conceal them, to the degree that she/he can accept their own anger, the pastor's own behavior presents a useful model for others. A pastor's fear of the depth or effects of his/her own angry feelings will react repressively to conflict among others as a function of the pastor's own defensiveness. Anger that is expressed as it is experienced seldom has the commonly feared potential for destruction inherent in anger which is warehoused until an offensive event sparks an uncontainable explosion.

Ultimately, the acceptance of one's anger as part of loving interpersonal relationships is a statement of faith. One may read the Crucifixion event as God's permission for the expression of anger by the provision of the Incarnational Self as the acceptable recipient. It is only after the Crucifixion, only after the anger is released, that reconciliation is possible! Without it, "the dividing wall of hostility"[1] would remain and the One whose nature it is to love and the beloved creation would be unable to move beyond into the possibility of intimacy that comes with the Spirit only after the Resurrection. And because anger is a recurrent experience, the wise provision of the symbolic means for its periodic re-enactment in the breaking of the bread leads us again into oneness. The verbal theological proclamation of the efficacy of this event will *only* become believable as it is consistent with the observable behavior of pastor in relationship to people. Training in conflict management and resolution for the pastor must be seen in its theological context so that what is implicit may become usefully explicit as the distinctive addition of the pastor to the work of the secular therapist. Integration of conflict management and resolution into all facets of pastoral care gives reality to the notion that God can handle anger and use it creatively and redemptively. Only then will we grasp what Jesus meant when he told his hearers that he came not to bring peace, but to bring a sword.[2]

NEEDED: THE PRIMACY OF GRACE

The increase in the number of older persons will confront the pastor with an even greater need to develop a theology in which worth and acceptance does not depend upon productivity. Faith proclamation and interpersonal response must become both inherently and behaviorally consistent. Most theologies, and therefore most preaching, contain a strong undercurrent of closet works righteousness. Theological fundamentalism is easily defended against because of the relative transparency of its ordering of grace as secondary to human action. More troublesome are the more "liberal" theologies because their stand on this issue is less clear, far more subtle, than pietistic legalism. An inner ambivalence that goes unresolved often cannot live comfortably with its testimony to the unconditional primacy of grace and finds itself appending conditions. Faith is equated with action and commitment with doing. Because of the impact of our human experience, it is enormously difficult to really believe the Good News of the gift of salvation without retaining a strong residue of suspicion that it surely cannot be true. This doubt, often unrecognized, gets communicated to our people. Younger Christians can continue, even though fruitlessly, to play the game of relating their accomplishments to their acceptability to God. This fits with their approaches to their careers, their social networks and often even their family relationships. Older Christians, who may no longer have the means nor the desire to play the game, search about for another way to understand themselves and their lives. When we arrive at the moment in life that unmasks the transience of achievement and works, life itself drives us back to grace. The clarity of this encounter with the all loving God is subject to confusion by the Church's message when it insists on works as a prerequisite, which the elderly have already discovered are ultimately empty, or when its ambivalence communicates the need for works as the proof of faith, which the elderly may no longer be able to enact. If God cannot love me without my commitment to Christ as a prerequisite or without my service to others as the outcome of faith, what about the senile old man who stares off into space and can no longer exert effective control of even the most elementary bodily functions? The extreme conditions of the aged call our theologies into effective judgement.

The theology of aging has been all but neglected. Except for Seward Hiltner's preliminary volume,[3] there is little available that addresses the question of what the meaning of the aging experience is in the creation of God. I suspect that the later years of life have purposes within them that need exposition and that would transcend the current emphasis upon death and dying. We must not spend the later years of life dying or preparing for death. They have an integrity of their own. They call upon us to live on levels that may be reserved for these years . . . not abandon life to a preoccupation with death. If death and dying are the last stage in life, we might do well to separate old age out into the preceding stage. Perhaps that would help us more adequately focus upon it. As there are some things that one cannot fully understand until you've been there, are there some insights available to the maturing Christian only in the last years of life? And, perhaps more importantly, how does the living of these later days contribute to our completion as the person God has created us to be?

The epigenetic model of human development suggests that the last years of life are a time to achieve a sense of integrity, or alternately, experience profound despair over the life that we have lived. Each of us mirrors God's own experience of looking back over what we have created and assessing that creation. The implication seems to be that the reflective task is oriented toward the past. And there needs to be some of that. But I wonder if we've not overlooked the call to look at what we are creating even in the final years and reflecting upon its meaning? Are there lessons we are learning even – or perhaps, only – now? Can enforced dependency teach us anything about life? Community? Ourselves? Our relationship with God? Can increased physical limitations teach us the ministry of receiving help? Is pride finally relegated to its appropriate place in life? And if so, what may we yet discover about life? Does prolonged illness impose the kinds of stress that prepare us to become more willing to deliver our lives into the embrace of the loving God? Might it be that the exhaustion that results from long-term illnesses is itself a way of preparing us to welcome death?

The questions are many and the opportunity to explore may be the gift that old age was meant to provide all along. We must turn to the aged themselves for guidance in this inquiry. I suspect that only they may really know. For them, the life that calls for reflection and assessment is not of the past but of the present! It is an opportunity to find God's grace even now. And out of careful attention to their reports of their experience in this latter stage of their lives may come the theology of aging that we presently lack. In fact, the ministry of listening to the aged may be the most important pastoral ministry in the decades ahead.

NOTES

1. Ephesians 2:14.
2. Matthew 10:34.
3. Seward Hiltner, *Toward a Theology of Aging* (New York: Human Sciences Press, 1975).

Biomedical Ethics in the Year 2000: O = f(H.E.F.)

Carl D. Chambers, PhD
Kathryn S. Pribble, MHSA
Michael T. Harter, PhD

SUMMARY. The elderly are disproportionate consumers of health care resources. The major burden for these health care costs is being borne by the public. As more and more of our elderly live longer and consume even more of these finite resources, access to these resources will be restricted and they will be placed at ever increasing levels of risk. The history, current status, and future "projections" for elderly health and health care access are presented.

INTRODUCTION

In order to save time for some of our readers, we have decided to make a number of personal and professional biases known "up front." We do this in recognition of both our inability and unwillingness to be completely dispassionate or totally objective when discussing what "we" are doing to and for our elders today or what "we" have in store for them in the future. While even we probably do not know or appreciate *all* of our biases, we do openly acknowledge these:

Carl D. Chambers is Professor and Coordinator of all Health Services Administration programs for Ohio University. He is also Director of the Gerontology Certificate Program, Chairs the University Committee on Aging and is a Licensed Nursing Home Administrator. Kathryn S. Pribble is a Licensed Recreational Therapist and Nursing Home Administrator. She recently completed her professional degree in Health Services Administration at Ohio University. Michael T. Harter is Acting Dean for the College of Health and Human Services at Ohio University and is Associate Professor in the graduate Health Services Administration Program.

47

1. When we first became aware of the book *Too Old, Too Sick, Too Bad* by Moss and Halamandaris a decade ago, we were intellectually disturbed. As we became programmatically active with the elderly, we were emotionally disturbed. We remain disturbed at both levels today.

2. While we are delightfully amazed at the marvelous extension of life expectancy we have seen in only a generation or so, we are unabashedly concerned about the quality of life these increased years have engendered. While our elders have indeed been given more years to live, they may not have "won." As a group, elders have not become happier, healthier, or more financially secure.

3. We believe that the quality of one's "golden years" is to a large extent determined by the prevalence and intensity of *fear*. For most of our elderly, daily living activities are played out on a stage where fear is a primary motivator. These include the fear of being old and ill, the fear of being poor and a burden, the fear of change and uncertainty, the fear of insanity, the fear of losing liberty, identity, and human dignity, the fear of poor care and abuse, and the fear of death. Further, we believe that the fears being perceived are real, being grounded in an accurate interpretation of what is happening to them and around them. These fears being felt by most of our elders indeed are rational, not irrational.

4. For most of our elders, social death, that loss of identity, freedom, and independence with the forced divestiture of dignity, precedes their physical death. They know this because they see it happening. The elderly will always strive to keep these two "deaths" as close together as possible and indeed rely upon those who care for them or advocate for them to assist them in this endeavor.

With at least our intellectual integrity intact, we can now begin to contemplate what specific biomedical and other related ethical issues are most likely to confront the elderly in our society during the year 2000. As we do so, we find ourselves engaging in the same intellectual and emotional exercises used by all who would predict the future. . . . Where have we come from? Where are we now? Has the journey to date established any patterns or trends which are likely to continue into the future? Should we, or could we, put strategies in place whereby we might decrease the risk of some negatives occurring and increase the probability of some positives occurring?

BIOMEDICAL ETHICS AND THE ELDERLY: YESTERDAY

As we begin to contemplate health care and other services for the elderly, we are reminded of the extraordinary advances which have been made by the medical sciences in our lifetime. By instituting major public health procedures, and through the development of the antibiotics and other medications, virtually all of the infectious diseases were eradicated. *In our lifetime, life expectancy has increased by almost two decades.* While everyone would applaud the decreases in premature death and the increase in longevity, their appearance produced some significant changes in our society. When we didn't have an elderly population, we didn't have to spend a great deal of time worrying about the quality of their lives nor concern ourselves with how they as a group would impact the overall distribution of resources including health care.

While laymen and some academics will periodically wax on about the "good old days" when the elderly enjoyed an accepted and functioning role within the extended family, any serious scholar would be hard pressed to find where and when such an idyllic situation existed for the majority of the elderly. For those who yearn to return to these more simple, more pleasant times, we refer them to Otto Bettmann's social commentary which bears a haunting realistic title, *The Good Old Days: They Were Terrible*. It is our analysis the elderly have been generally *tolerated* in our society as long as they were capable of working and contributing to both their own support and to the common good. Once the mass migration into this country began to crowd our cities and once the population shifted from an agrarian to an industrial work force, the elderly were at increased risk for becoming alienated and dependent. A recognition of this alienation and dependency is reflected in major pieces of social legislation which emerged after the Great Depression of the 1930s:

- The passage of the Social Security Act of 1935 attempted to address the special needs of the elderly. The intent of this legislation was to provide *some* measure of economic security to the nation's workers and their families. By 1985, more than nine out of ten workers in this country were a contributing part of this "retirement" program and some 93 percent of all our elders were drawing some benefit from this program.
- The passage of the 1960 Kerr-Mills Amendment to the Social Security Act was the first legislation to recognize that the el-

derly might have *specific* need for help in financing their health care cost. This amendment, the forerunner of the present Medicaid program, provided assistance to those elderly citizens who by circumstance were forced to be "medically indigent."

• In 1965 two new amendments were added to the Social Security Act, which brought into focus the special health care needs of the elderly. A comprehensive health insurance package became available for the first time for every older citizen (Title XVIII: Medicare). *Medicare* is available to everyone over age 65 and it has two "parts." Part A is an insurance program which provides basic hospitalization coverage plus coverage for some post-hospital services. Reimbursements payable under this "third-party" payment system are subject to deductible payments and co-insurance payments by the elderly not dissimilarly seen with private carriers. The second part of the Medicare program (Part B) is an optional program which the elderly can purchase providing basic coverage for physician charges. As with the hospitalization coverages, the physician coverage is subject to deductible and co-insurance payments by the elderly beneficiary. Additionally, a major medical assistance program for the medically indigent, including older citizens, was implemented (Title XIX: Medicaid).

• A final piece of major social legislation which impacted the lives of some elders was enacted in 1975, also as an amendment to the Social Security Act. This Title XX Amendment authorizes federal reimbursement to states for providing citizens, including elders, who are income-eligible with certain social services. This assistance is designed to help those who are still independently residing in the community in the hopes they do not become fully dependent or institutionalized.

The intent was to insure elderly citizens an equitable share of our collective resources, including health care. The process of accumulating monies into trusts which would generate interest income to distribute to beneficiaries is a generally accepted way of financing such "insurance" programs. Policy makers and special interest groups all saw these *legislation interventions* as examples of our collective conscience at work and as the realization of distributive justice in health and human services. Unfortunately, neither the policy makers nor the special interest advocates came to grips intellectually with what has to occur when one attempts to address infinite needs with finite resources. They would have done so.

BIOMEDICAL ETHICS AND THE ELDERLY: TODAY

> . . . whatever one feels is right—or wrong—about American society today can be illustrated by health care.[1]

The Older Americans Act of 1965 is that benchmark legislation which established the baseline expectations of elders and their advocates with regard to the equitable distribution of various resources. *This act seemed to set forth equitable distribution as rights inherent to the elderly.* Consider the meaning and implications of the opening declaration of this 1965 legislation:

> The congress hereby finds and declares that, in keeping with the traditional American concept of the inherent dignity of the individual in our democratic society, the older people of our Nation are entitled to, and it is the joint and several duty and responsibility of the governments of the United States and of several States and their political subdivisions to assist our older people to secure equal opportunity to the full and free enjoyment of the following objectives:
>
> 1. An adequate income in retirement in accordance with the American standard of living.
> 2. The best possible physical and mental health which science can make available and without regard to economic status.
> 3. Suitable housing, independently selected, designed and located with reference to special needs and available at costs which older citizens can afford.
> 4. Full restorative services for those who require institutional care.
> 5. Opportunity for employment with no discriminatory personnel practices because of age.
> 6. Retirement in health, honor, dignity—after years of contribution to the economy.
> 7. Pursuit of meaningful activity within the widest range of civic, cultural, and recreational activities.

8. Efficient community services which provide social assistance in a coordinated manner and which are readily available when needed.
9. Immediate benefit from proven research knowledge which
   can sustain and improve health and happiness.
10. Freedom, independence, and the free exercise of individ-
    ual initiative in planning and managing their own lives.

With the passage of this landmark legislation, distributive justice
had finally arrived for our elders! Or had it? Most of the elderly
were eligible for at least minimal Social Security pension benefits.
Medicare was in place for virtually everyone. Medicaid was in place
for the medically indigent. But, we were not quite there. We needed
the Title XX Amendment to the Social Security Act to fill in gaps in
other human service areas for those who needed these services but
could not afford to purchase them. Now our elderly could retire
without fear. Or could they? Unfortunately, while Congress has always seemed willing to establish the expectations and to place the
basic mechanisms in place to address these expectations, it has
never seen fit to provide the funding necessary to meet and sustain
these expressed objectives. WE NOW KNOW THAT SOME ARE
IMPOSSIBLE AND MOST ARE IMPROBABLE SOLELY FROM
THE STANDPOINT OF ECONOMIC REALITIES AND OVER-
EXTENDED PRIORITIES.

Although many elders are certainly better off today than they
were twenty years ago when these major social programs were initi-
ated, there are many others who remain largely untouched by these
legislative initiatives. Significant health and human service needs
continue to persist among our elders. Moreover, during the past five
years, public funding of health and human service programs for
elders has been cut by at least 40 percent in constant dollar
amounts.[2] The cutting of these programs has caused the emergence
of a *two-tiered health and human service system* that in effect denies
vital care and other supports to the non-affluent elder. Those who do
not have constant contact with the elderly population frequently un-
derestimate the impact of such a system. For example, studies of the
economic status of older Americans indicate that about 3.3 million
are below the poverty line, with an additional 2.2 million "near
poor." The two groups combined represent more than 25 percent of
all elders. The lack of sufficient retirement income is without question one of the most critical issues affecting the emotional and phys-

ical well-being of our elderly citizens. For that subset of elders who face problems both from poor health and inadequate income, these problems too often have a ruinous compound impact. THE AVERAGE INCOME FOR THE ELDERLY IS BETWEEN 50 AND 60 PERCENT OF THAT FOR THE GENERAL POPULATION BUT MEDICAL BILLS AT AGE 65 ARE THREE TO FOUR TIMES HIGHER THAN WHEN THE OLDER PERSON WAS YOUNGER. At the very time when one's purchasing power is less than half of what it was, medical expenses multiply by a factor of three. Is it any wonder that among the elders' catalogue of fears, becoming ill and being too poor to secure adequate care are the two that are most prominent.[3]

In 1977, per capita health care spending for persons 65 years of age and over was, on the average, 3.5 times that for the total population.[4] That ratio is even higher today and is expected to continue to rise in spite of the cost containment activities currently in place. Per capita health care expenditures have been increasing at a rate considerably in excess of overall inflation. For example, the increase between 1977 and 1978 was 13 percent.[5] Total health care expenditures on the elderly are expected to rise from about $50 billion in 1978 to amost $200 billion in 2000, in constant 1980 dollars.[6]

Health care costs for the elderly are underwritten as shown in the following proportional distribution.[7]

Medicare..............................	50%
Medicaid..............................	13%
Other Government Programs........	5%
Private Insurers......................	7%
Elderly "out-of-pockets"............	25%

Thus, in excess of two-thirds of the current health care expenditures on the elderly are being borne through public (government) programs. The federally financed Medicare program bears the "lion's share" of health care costs. Current and projected deficits in this program keep its soundness and actual survival in constant jeopardy. In 1984 the Health Care Financing Administration projected the Medicare trust fund could be exhausted as early as 1989 if the current laws, reimbursement practices, and coverages were not modified.[8] Our best 1985 estimate is that a 20 percent increase in taxes or a 20 percent decrease in disbursements, or any combination of the two, is required just to remain even for the remainder of the decade.

In recent years, we have seen more and more of the costs being shifted to the elderly consumer through higher premiums, deductibles, and co-payments. As the "public" monies become more threatened, this shift will undoubtedly accelerate.

For the very young being ill is a transitory problem. For the old, being well is generally just as transitory. For most people, being old *means* having health problems that don't go away . . . one's health problems are chronic and progressively debilitating, necessitating constant and ever increasing health care resource utilization.

One would assume this situation will only get "worse" because the number of people who survive to become elderly is increasing and the pool of the very old is increasing even more rapidly. *We are becoming older but not healthier.*

For example, a number of studies have concluded that a significant portion of the population ages 65 and above is *not* in good health.[9] More specifically the *current* population of older persons presents as:

- 30 percent are in no better than fair health.
- 22 percent are experiencing limitations in their major daily living activities due to their health.
- 18 percent are unable to carry out their major daily living activities unassisted due to their health.
- Each elderly person averages 13 bed disability days per year because of poor health.
- On any given day, the "average" elderly person will report 1.1 acute health problems and 3.3 chronic ones.

From the perspectives of trying to determine current or to predict future biomedical issues, it is most important to appreciate the fact that being in poor health and needing access to health care is *not* equally distributed among our elderly population. For example, these same studies have established major differences by age, residence, and socioeconomic status.

- Those who are above age 70 report significantly more poor health than those under age 70 (55 percent versus 33 percent).
- The urban elderly report significantly more poor health than the rural elderly (55 percent versus 45 percent).
- Among the elderly poor, some 60 percent report poor health.

Thus, if the current pattern persists into the year 2000 when the elderly population is even *more weighted* in the direction of urban poor over age 70, the debates surrounding distributive justice in health care and other human services will be even more predominant than they have been.

BIOMEDICAL ETHICS
AND THE ELDERLY: TOMORROW

Predicting *some* of the major concerns with biomedical ethics and the elderly seems to be a fairly straightforward process. For example, we would suggest the following will require a rather formal forum for discussion.

In spite of major legislation and other policy interventions, we believe concerns among the elderly and their advocates about the *equitable distribution of health and human services resources* will be one of the dominant unresolved ethical issues in the year 2000. Needs will continue to expand at alarming rates due to increasing pressures from additional longevity in the population generally, increasing pressures from the therapies required for long term management of chronic debilitating conditions coupled with periodic acute episodes, and from the technological advances which can be expected to enter the marketplace and generate a new wave of demands and additional consumption.

The elderly in this country made a fundamental mistake in their pursuit of distributive justice with respect to health and human services resources. Their needs were too great. Their "fair share" of the resources based upon demonstrable needs was more than the "system" seemed willing or able to commit for their specific use. While it was emotionally, philosophically, and politically appropriate to talk about health and other human services as if they were "rights," it seems obvious to us now that they never really could be. If rights dictated the distribution of the limited resources disproportionately to those who had the greatest need, we would have to cope with the problem of too few people being left to shoulder the cost for the too many people who were consuming the benefits. Economic self-interest would seem to preclude such a system succeeding.

The reality of the situation is that the elderly were, are, and will continue to be primary consumers of our limited health and human service resources. At a time when the elderly comprised only 12 percent of the total population, they were already consuming one-third of our total health care resources. Two-thirds of the cost burden for this disproportionate consumption of these services is in *public dollars*.[11] If one assumes a situation where there is virtually infinite needs but finite resources, the debate is not on whether to "ration" access to resources, but rather it is where the rationing should be imposed. We believe the elderly are especially vulnerable for restricted access through rationing. Consider the devastating cost/benefit arguments which would ensue when the following sequence of "facts" relative to the elderly and their "disproportionate" consumption of limited health care resources should become widely known:

- 93 percent of all elderly persons are covered by Medicare.
- Medicare pays for 50 percent of all elderly health care costs.
- A subset of about 25 percent of all the elders consumed about 75 percent of all the Medicare resources. These tended to be the older and poorer of the elders.
- In 1985, Medicare paid out $65 billion for elderly health care costs.
- In 1985, Medicare paid out $20 billion (almost one-third of all costs) for care for the elderly during the last year of their lives.
- In 1985, Medicare paid out $6 billion (some 10 percent of all payments) for care for the elderly during the last month of their lives.

In 1967, Medicare payment for beneficiaries was only about $4 billion. In less than twenty years, it had grown to $65 billion. Reductions in benefits, increases in payroll taxes to support the program, increases in deductibles, and increases in co-payments are almost annual attempts at curtailing the consumption and protecting the resource. None would appear to have been especially successful.

It is somewhat frightening to speculate what discussions will surface by the year 2000 when our elderly population has doubled in size and contains a higher proportion of the sick old elderly (age 85 and above). Health and human service demands unquestionably will have increased at least proportionately. Some form of rationing, therefore, seems inevitable. One can only hope we see the basic morality of directing this rationing, by rationing *away* from those with fewer needs and/or more private resources while rationing *toward* those with more needs and/or fewer private resources to meet them.

One should anticipate the elderly will be called upon to increase their "fair share" of the monetary burden of providing the health care they actually consume or are at risk for consuming. Most analysts project the elderly are already spending around 10 percent of their total available incomes for direct purchases of health care services or for the purchasing of third-party coverage in anticipation of the services they will be needing. Certainly it is not inconceivable that this contribution could explode to about 25 percent by the year 2000. The historical trend to higher deductibles, higher co-payment purchase premiums for catastrophic and other supplemental coverage makes such a projection believable. To date, every time there has been an impending insolvency in the Medicare Funds, either through decreasing contributions or increasing distributions to beneficiaries, purchase prices and deductibles have risen. With *fewer workers* to make contributions to the funds and *greater numbers of beneficiaries* consuming resources for greater lengths of time, the end result is predictable. While these increases in proportional cost burden will affect the lifestyles of the elderly, the major problem does not emerge until which time the specific older person is unable to purchase basic Part B coverage, to purchase supplemental coverage, to pay the initial deductible either for Part A or Part B, or to pay directly for needed services. In times of need and the absence of resources, who pays? . . . What will happen to even the current level of restricted access? The reader is asked to remember, QUESTIONS OF ACCESS ARE NORMALLY DEBATED AROUND THOSE WHO ARE UNABLE TO PAY, NOT AROUND THOSE WHO HAVE ACCUMULATED THE RESOURCES TO PURCHASE DIRECTLY OR INDIRECTLY. The outcome of this process will be that the two-tiered health and human service system which emerged during the early 1980's as a result of a wide variety of economic pressures will become galvanized.

We believe the debate over *cost versus benefit* will continue into the year 2000. The economic realities of "finite resources" will make this necessary. Rationing demands may force us to restrict access to those who are known to be terminal or whose prognosis includes the anticipation of a severely impaired level of existence or vegetative state as the patient's outcome.

It would appear we have come to accept the "right" of the person who is emotionally stable and intellectually intact to be significantly involved in his or her treatment decisions. Most of us have become comfortable with the notion that "competent" persons have the right to reject treatment altogether. But there is much less consensus about what should become of those people who are not "competent" to decide their own fates. Discussions about *who* should decide, *when* the decisions should be made, and *how* this process should occur and be monitored have been generally unsatisfactory to date. Hopefully by the year 2000, our society will have come to grips with the inevitability of death. Up until this time, we seem to have confused our efforts at prolonging dying with our quest to prolong life. It seems to us that we have replaced the natural death process with a system driven by both death-delaying technology and a death-delaying social ethic. Biomedical arguments should continue to abound concerning what we owe as human beings to other human beings who are going to die and what are the rational limits to the use of medical technology. Perhaps the concept too often heard among our medical colleagues . . . we can't do nothing . . . will become much less prevalent. Indeed, it may become acceptable to do nothing.

However, it seems unlikely the ethical debates surrounding the full euthanasia issue will be resolved by the year 2000. While "active" euthanasia models will continue to surface around us, such as a terminally ill patient choosing to ask the physician to directly end his or her life or where a "mercy killing" occurs, we would expect that health care professionals will continue within the traditional precept of treating the patient as if he/she valued life above all else and that that life should be protected at all costs. However, the more "passive" euthanasia models may be more open to discussion. For example, there may be pressures to accept the ideas of withdrawing life-support measures at the request of a terminally ill patient, there may be pressures to restrict the use of aggressive therapies and/or extraordinary measures with several categories of patients with "poor" prognoses or where "desirable" outcomes are unlikely, and maybe there will be pressures to withdraw the life-support measures from comatose or vegetative state patients even when there is no indication of present or past request to do so. Passive euthanasia is already an option for some of those who remain competent through the time of the request. We believe that this will be extended to include some categories of those who are not competent to make their wishes known. Many families already negotiate this outcome with the physician of their loved one. Euthanasia, both active and passive, may become the individual's *last* right.

We would suggest one of the major biomedical ethical debates will emerge over the issues of experimentation and informed consent. It is astonishing just how little we know about the aging process itself, let alone how to retard it, how to account for it in our treating processes, or how to reverse it. Consider once again what will happen by the year 2020 when roughly 20 percent of our population will be above the age of 65 with major growth being in the age group above age 85. All of these "old people" will bring their "old people's diseases and conditions" with them to present them to a medical community who poorly understands them. What therapies will the physician choose to use? What medications are available which have also undergone clinical trials with the geriatric population? What new things can be tried "just" on the chance "it" will work? Physician experimentation on the elderly is likely to occur both out of a desire to practice medicine better and out of a desire to hide one's ignorance. While all of us appreciate the need to accumulate new knowledge, we must also appreciate the need to protect the rights of the elderly patient. This will require some very careful definitions about just *what is therapeutic medicine and what is experimental medicine*, as well as just what is informed consent from someone who is in chronic pain from multiple physical problems, who is suffering major metabolic imbalances, who is symptomatically responding to a wide variety of medications, and who is under untold psychological distress. Our own experiences would suggest that what is frequently being "sold" as aggressive therapy with our elders is in reality experimental medicine being practiced without fully informed consent. Sooner or later, the debates must focus on whether truly informed consent is even possible in most debilitated terminal patients. And, indeed, we must decide if most aggressive therapies are defensible.

By the year 2000 it will have become obvious to everyone that some form of "public" regulation of the impending proprietary domination of the health care delivery system will be required. How much regulation should be imposed, upon whom, by whom, and when will require considerable debate. In the absence of regulation, the free enterprise portion of the system will likely be directed by an aggressive competition for the most cost effective patient to the exclusion of the others. If this is permitted to happen, the elderly will find themselves at a major disadvantage for securing services. While there are some major advantages to having private for-profit ownership and control of the health care industry, some safeguards to protect the elderly and other disadvantaged or vulnerable consumers will be required. We have some concern that the proprietary groups will not only "own" the delivery system, they will also be in control of the major research and teaching facilities. When this occurs, they will also be in a position to demand first choice use of any technological advances, advanced techniques and procedures, and experimental drug therapies. Equitable access for the elderly may become even more difficult and more of an ethical concern than it is today.

CONCLUSION

$$O = f(H.E.F.)$$

As we have marched through time from "yesterday" through "today" to "tomorrow"; we have come to realize that the predominant biomedical ethical issue has been and will continue to be centered around distributive justice . . . equitable distribution of limited resources. We see the elderly of 2000 as being very vulnerable and poorly equipped to compete for limited health and human resources. In fact, we see both the concept and the reality of *old* (O) as a function (f) of one's *health status* (H), one's *economic status* (E), and one's *level of fear* (F). For some, being old is a detriment. For others, "golden years" is a reality.

As long as one's health is poor . . . one's economic status is poor . . . one's level of fear is high . . . the more "needs" one will have and the greater the likelihood that these needs will not be met. If our elders are to receive distributive justice, a new model for making this happen will have to be found. In fact, if our elders are to live with health, honor, dignity, and independence and if they are to be able to die with honor and dignity, a whole array of new ethical, intellectual, economic, and service delivery models will have to be found. Our society tried very hard between 1965 and 1985 to find these new models and did not succeed. Hopefully, by the year 2000, we will have at least some progress.

NOTES

1. C. Levine, "Ethics and Health Cost Containment." In *The Hasting Center Report*, 9 (1979), pp. 10-13.

2. See editorial comments by J. Nathanson in the September-October, 1985 edition of *The Connection*, the bimonthly newspaper of the American Society of Aging, on the occasion of his election to the presidency of the Society.

3. F. Moss and V. Halamandaras, *Too Old, Too Sick, Too Bad*, Germantown, 1977.

4. While this figure is quoted widely, an excellent summary is contained in C. Carl Pegels, *Health Care and the Elderly*, Rockville, 1981 and in C. Fisher, "Differences by Age Groups in Health Care Spending," *Health Care Financing Review*, Spring, 1980.

5. D. Waldo and H. Lozenby, "Demographic Characteristics and Health Care Use and Expenditures by the Aged in the United States," *Health Care Financing Review*, 6 (1984), pp. 1-29.

6. K. Davis, "The Medical Care Challenge of an Aging Population," *Statistical Bulletin*, April-June (1984), p. 13.

7. Waldo and Lozenby, *op. cit.* pp. 10-11.

8. *Ibid.*, p. 27.

9. For several analyses confirming these data, see T. Tissue, "The survey of the Low-Income Aged and Disabled: An Introduction," in *Social Security Bulletin* 40, 1972, pp. 3-11; K. F. Ferraro, "Self-Rating of Health Among the Old and the Old-Old," *Journal of Health and Social Behavior*, 21 (1980), pp. 377-383; C. Chambers, *A Report of the Physical and Mental Health Status and Therapy Index for the General Population*, Geneva, Fla., 1980 (Unpublished); C. Chambers, *A Report of the Physical and Mental Health Status for the Residents in Southeast Ohio*, Athens, Ohio, 1982 (Unpublished); C. Chambers, O. White, J. Linquist, and M. Harter, "Patterns and Correlates of Minor Tranquilizer Use Within a Tri-Ethnic Population of the Noninstitutionalized Elderly," paper presented at the Southwestern Sociological Association Annual Meeting, 1984 (unpublished); Waldo and Lozenby, *op. cit.*, pp. 8-9; C. Chambers and K. Pribble, "Health Status of the Elderly: Infinite Need and Finite Resources," in *The Elderly: Victims and Deviants*, Athens, Ohio (in press).

10. R. Morison, "Bioethics After Two Decades," in *The Hasting Center Report*" (1981), pp. 8-11.

11. For two analyses which confirm these data, see Waldo and Lozenby, *op. cit.*, pp. 10-11, and the Surgeon General's report, "Healthy Older Adults," *Healthy People*, Washington, D.C. (1979), pp. 71-76.

Death:
The Inevitable Issue

Lindsey P. Pherigo, PhD

SUMMARY. In the near future there will be some changes in our patterns of dying, but only in superficial and circumstantial ways. The present views of what death is and what causes natural death probably will not change. The brightest prospects for new learnings about death are from the new physics and the new metaphysics it has produced, and possibly from scientifically respectable psychic data.

There's an effective scene in the motion picture "The Man from Snowy River" in which a young man unduly laments the accidental death of his father. The rough-hewn philosopher, Spooner, finally rebukes him back into the world of reality by the terse comment, "There's more to life than death, Jim." That's certainly true, and for most of us concern for the quality of our life is more immediately important than our concern for things that have to do with our death. But death is eventually top-priority for all of us. What will future generations be thinking when they contemplate the meaning of death?

Of all the changes ahead that have to do with dying, the most obvious are the circumstantial ones. Dying will tend to move out of the hospital and back into the home where it used to be.

Part of the reason for this will be purely practical. Hospital costs are spiraling up out of sight, and yet nothing, not even the fortunes of the very wealthy, succeeds in thwarting death, eventually. All expenses are, finally, futile. "All things of earth have an end . . . All the earth is a grave, and naught escapes it." [1]

Lindsey P. Pherigo is Professor Emeritus of New Testament and Early Church History at Saint Paul School of Theology in Kansas City, Missouri. His PhD is from Boston University in Church History. This article is one of a series of studies he has made in gerontological theology.

63

Another part of the reason for this return of dying to the home will be personal. There is something inhumane about the present isolation of the dying from their customary environment and the circle of their own intimates. There is an increasing sensitivity to the impersonal environment of the modern hospital. Dying in a society of technicians will give way to dying in the familiar surroundings of home and in the society of the family. The pioneering hospice movement is a clear indication of this trend, and it is only a beginning.

The modern hospice movement grew out of a special concern for the circumstances in which people live out a terminal illness and die. It says, in effect, "we are perfectly capable of handling . . . death by ourselves without the help of institutions."[2] It teaches people the basics of dying at home, and in doing so with increasing popularity the hospice movement documents a trend of the future.

Dying at home means that future generations will have more personal contact with death. The persons in pre-technological civilization, Alvin Toffler's "first wave,"[3] were familiar with death. This familiarity will return again in the "the third wave" now beginning. Experiences with the death of others will be restored to its more natural place, after its recent confinement to hospitals by the technological industrial civilization ("the second wave") now disintegrating, according to Toffler's analysis.

This more personal contact with death will, in turn, intensify "the problem of death." We will be less able in the future than we have in the recent past to ignore or repress the reality of death. Ernest Becker, in his Pulitzer Prize essay,[4] has brilliantly analyzed the problems created in second-wave civilization by its avoidance of the reality of death. Future generations will be in a renewed struggle to understand and deal with that reality this present generation has been accustomed to denying or ignoring.

One of the unsolved mysteries about death is, of course, why we die of "natural causes." Everyone understands the reason for a death that has an immediate cause, such as an accident or a disease that's fatal, but why do healthy old persons die? It will not do to think that "something" must have been present and causal that we did not know about. Death is certain, quite apart from those causes which bring it on earlier. Mastering the fatal disease will not conquer death, but only postpone the inevitable. As Lucretius observed in his most famous poem:

. . . Suppose you could contrive to live for centuries. As many as you will. Death, even so, will still be waiting for you. . . ."[5]

We have made great progress in extending life expectancy, and will undoubtedly make even more strides toward a new longevity. That increase in the time-span of "old-age" will give gerontologists much to do in their field, but this new longevity has nothing to do with death itself. Why do we die?

There are three popular explanations of "natural" death. Each has arisen out of its own special background, one from some form of belief in "fatalism," another from a "will of God" theology, and a third from the "wearing-out" syndrome.

Fatalism (in the West) goes back to popular theology in ancient Greece. In post-Homeric times three old women, "the Fates," were popularly believed to determine the life-span of each individual person. They were imaged as spinning out our lives on spinning wheels. Even the gods were powerless to change their "fatal" decrees. In our time this belief that our life-span is predetermined is still quite popular (without the Greek mythology), surfacing in cliches like "what will be, will be," or ideas like "if it isn't my time to die, nothing can kill me; if it is nothing can save me."

In the second of these currently popular explanations, it is God that determines our time of death. The "will of God" approach ascribes the course of history, including one's personal history, to a controlling God. God determines the main events of history, especially the central matters of life and death, much in the style of the ancient Hebrew God, Yahveh.

I am Yahveh, and there is no other.
I form light and create darkness,
I make weal and create woe,
I am Yahveh, who do all these things.[6]

Where this control is limited to our ultimate destiny, rather than to such relative matters as the length of our life, we enter the theological territory of "election" and "predestination." These, of course, should not be confused with fatalism.

The "wearing out" theme, the third explanation in our time, may be the most popular, currently. Everyone knows that manufactured things do "wear out." It is easy to transfer a familiar known to an unknown that seems parallel. In time, it is often thought, our vital organs just "wear out." If so, however, then we are rapidly approaching the time when we can replace them individually as they wear out. Transplants are increasingly successful, with organs from human and animal donors. We are on the edge of an era of successful transplants of artificial (man-made) organs. In the future we may be able to make the parts we need, and thus cultivate the illusion that we can eventually outwit death. But this is only an illusion; all we will be able to do is to extend life a bit and postpone the inevitable.

I personally believe that there is no future prospect of our doing anything more than increasing the life-span. Why? Because death is a feature of all life forms on this planet. The universality of death as the natural end of every life cycle precludes any "solution" to the problem of death itself. As a wise anonymous ancient Hebrew writer said:

> For everything there is a season
>   and a time for every matter under heaven
> A time to be born, and a time to die . . . [7]

I have found no new theory to explain natural death that seems likely to me. That our cells are genetically programmed to divide only so many times and then to stop dividing, bringing "natural death," seems far away from demonstration. And even if this theory turns out to have some basis, our future progress in gene-manipulation could enter the picture to alter the programming genes, at least in the direction of prolonging life.

In science fiction physical immortality is sometimes a theme, usually as an achievement of a more advanced science in some remote part of the universe. Even in science fiction though, the further question is raised. Is such physical immortality even desirable? Robert Heinlein's *Time Enough for Love* is a case in point. [8]

Our physical existence is no bed of roses to be eternally perpetuated. As strikingly phrased by Ernest Becker:

> Creation is a nightmare spectacle taking place on a planet that
> has been soaked for hundreds of millions of years in the blood

of its creatures. The soberest conclusion that we could make about what has actually been taking place on the planet for about three billion years is that it is being turned into a vast pit of fertilizer.[9]

Or, in a very effective portrayal of his own mother's death (from cancer), John Topolewski has transformed into narrative form how that final knock at the door was handled. The mother brushed aside all the pretenses and denials and ordered her sons, "Open the door and let him [Death] in."

> And there he stood.
> and he was changed.
> The ugly visage of the Angel of Death had been transformed into something, something oddly attractive—even beautiful. He came to our Mother and held out his hands. He offered two gifts, peace and rest. And then, on a day now remembered for both giving birth and dying, our Mother went with the Angel. [10]

Life as we know it is hardly deserving of an eternal status. Death has its proper place, not as the Enemy, but as the Final Friend. Hence the pessimistic Biblical comments: "wherefore I praised the dead which are already dead more than the living which are yet alive," and "the day of death [better] than the day of one's birth." [12] Or, in a different, more realistic vein, Jesus ben Sirach wrote

> O death, how bitter is the reminder of you
> to one who lives at peace among his possessions,
> to a man without distractions,
>   who is prosperous in everything,
>   who still has the vigor to enjoy his food!
> O death, how welcome is your sentence
> to one who is in need and is failing in strength,
> very old and distracted over everything;
> to one who is contrary, and has lost his patience.[13]

Perhaps the most rapturous praise of death was penned by Walt Whitman, near the close of his poem expressing his grief over the assassination of President Abraham Lincoln:

Come lovely and soothing death,
Undulate round the world, serenely arriving, arriving,
In the day, in the night, to all, to each,
Sooner or later delicate death.

Prais'd be the fathomless universe,
For life and joy, and for object and knowledge curious,
And for love, sweet love — but praise! praise! praise!
For the sure-enwinding arms of cool-enfolding death.

Dark mother always gliding near with soft feet,
Have none chanted for thee a chant of fullest welcome?
Then I chant it for thee I glorify thee above all,
I bring thee a song that when thou must indeed come,
come unfalteringly. [14]

Beyond the circumstantial changes ahead, and beyond the un-solved mysteries of the causes of natural death, we can attempt some projections about our increased personal control over death, and about how we will come to regard the meaning of death itself.

It seems clear to me that the immediate future will return to us individually more control over our own death than we have had recently. We lost some control in the wake of the technological age Toffler has called "the second wave." Both birth and death, in the developed aspects of second wave civilization, were taken from the immediacy of the family and set in the sterile and impersonal envi-ronment of the hospital. Every effort, usually at tremendous cost, was expended to keep persons alive. It was a strange development, given the inevitability of the outcome. Death always wins, and the most technology could do was to buy a little time. But the time thus bought was often not time that anyone, especially the dying person, found meaningful. We often extended only miserable living. The root idea governing this situation was (and still is) the idea of the sacredness of life *per se*, the intrinsic sacredness of life itself. This idea is now being reevaluated. The future will take more seriously some limitations on what life is sacred, moving toward some defini-tion of "meaningful existence," and giving us more control, at least, over our own death time. The "right to die with dignity" movement is waxing and the absoluteness of the idea of the sanctity of life itself is waning.

It has recently struck me as strangely biased that proponents of life-sanctity have traditionally (in the West) meant only human life. Animals and plants have no "right-to-life"; human life (sacred) is founded and perpetuated on the programmed death of animals and plants which are in the *prime* of *their* life. It is not life itself that we have set apart, but *human* life. Perspectives are now enlarging. Future generations will see life in its larger context. This will reduce the special sanctity of human life itself, and increase our (proper) concern for the rights of animals to co-exist on this planet.

We humans in the future will be reconsidering the ethics of suicide and euthanasia. Individuals may gain the right to decide when to die. A beginning of this can be seen in the "living will" statutes now appearing in a few states. In cases where personal preferences have already been clearly and legally established, future generations may be able to make decisions about the death of a loved one when that loved one has gone beyond the decision-making stage into a painful or meaningless existence. There will be much hassle here, both ethical and legal, but it will come in the wake of the individualization being brought in by "the third wave."

If these are forecastings for our changing attitudes toward our control over our own death, what about the deeper concern about death itself? What *is* death? Is it the end of personal existence, or a transition into a different kind of existence? What will we think in the future about what is beyond death, if anything?

Basic to this is the question of defining a human being. Western Christianity has traditionally and popularly adopted the Orphic-Platonic definition. We humans are dualistic in "nature," with the soul of spirit (or, to use current psychological language, the "self"), distinct from the physical body it inhabits. In this view the body is not ultimately part of the real "self." In our essence, we are naturally immortal "souls" ("selves"), temporarily housed in a physical body. In my opinion this popularly established viewpoint is not likely to be abandoned in the near future, at least.

Why not? Because it explains better than other hypotheses our common experience. We feel our body and yet we feel something that does not seem to be our body. Our body determines much of our life activities, yet we feel that we are something that transcends the body. Among all the outward and undeniable signs of inevitable physical death, there are "Intimations of Immortality." This vague sense is widely expressed in the literature of all ages, even in the sacred literature of the Hebrews, which is not dualistic in the Orphic-Platonic sense. An ancient Hebrew sage noted, regretfully, that

God has " . . . put eternity into man's mind, yet so that he cannot find out what God has done. . . . "[15]

Ernest Becker, in *The Denial of Death*, takes this dualistic viewpoint uncritically as the simple truth that everyone knows. He calls attention to the "essential paradox." A human being is a "symbolic self" which gives to him or her "literally the status of a small god in nature," yet is also "a worm and food for worms." The human body is "a material fleshly casing that is alien to him in many ways . . . Man is literally split in two . . . a terrifying dilemma to be in and to have to live with."[16]

An alternative viewpoint, however, is both older than this dualistic view given classical expression by Plato, and yet it is more recent also.

The older alternative form is expressed in the Hebrew Bible. There human beings are not a dualistic paradox but a unity. Of course, the thought of these ancient Hebrews was little more than a naive assumption, and not a carefully thought-out analysis. They shared uncritically the common view of ancient Mediterranean and Mesopotamian cultures that a "shadow" or "shade" of the original person survived and went into the Land of the Dead (Sheol, Tartaros, Anwat, Orcus, Hades, Gehenna, etc.). This was the destiny of all persons. This was not a kind of immortality in the later Greek sense, for it was far from being an escape of our true essence from a bodily prison into a better form of existence. For all practical purposes the ancients regarded death as the end of meaningful existence. No body, no real life, they assumed.

To cite Lucretius again:

> So, when we cease to be, and body and soul,
> which joined to make us one, have gone their ways,
> their separate ways, nothing at all can shake
> our feelings, not if earth were mixed with sea
> or sea with sky. Perhaps the mind or spirit,
> after its separation from our body,
> Has some sensation; what is that to us?
> Nothing at all, for what we knew of being,
> Essence, identity, oneness, was derived
> From body's union with spirit . . . [17]

The body is thus not a temporary housing for the soul, in this viewpoint, but an essential ingredient in the makeup of a human being. Believing this, the requirements of divine justice led the Hebrews to adopt (probably from the Persians) a belief in a future resurrection (of both body and "soul") specifically for the purpose of conferring providentially promised rewards and punishments in a Last Judgment.

The modern form of this, often claiming (wrongly) continuity with the ancient Hebrew view (and, incidentally, authority from the Bible), is usually expressed by some use of the new word "holistic." A human being, in this understanding, is a complex of body, mind, emotions, and spirit. There cannot be a full human being without all of its "parts." When this holistic approach is consistently carried to its logical conclusion, death is the end of meaningful personhood. My observations, however, lead me to speculate that most of the holistic ideologists of our time do not, and will not in the future, carry this theme out to its logical conclusion. They seem content to believe that a holistic approach is needed for life before death, and what death really is can be left an open question. I personally think the dualistic view will maintain its present hold on the popular mind in the foreseeable future.

New speculations about death itself have come mostly from two sources. One of them is rooted in the new physics, and the other is the more controversial area of "extra-sensory-perception," or "psychic phenomena," or "parapsychology."

An almost untouched area of investigation has been created by the new physics. This new physics is so recent that only a few fields of knowledge are studying its implications for their discipline. Philosophers cannot ignore it, and the new physics has produced a new metaphysics in the pioneering work of Alfred North Whitehead. This in turn has produced a new theology, called "process theology."

A lesser beginning has been made in psychology and pastoral care, mostly under the influence of the inescapable impact of Whitehead's metaphysics. Gerontologists have not been significantly influenced because they are not primarily concerned with what death is, but rather with problems and issues that bear directly on the elderly segment of the population while they (the elderly) are still alive.

What has the new physics done to create a new area for investigation? It has made us aware that matter and energy are different forms of the same reality, and that space and time are not different qualitatively but are on a continuum. Physics has begun to document what imaginative science fiction writers have previsioned. We are now forced to acknowledge the limitations of human perceptions, and that the "real world" is much larger than the part we can perceive.

We commonly acknowledge this now in areas like sonic wave lengths beyond our range of hearing, and the way X-rays and various kinds of light ("infra-red," "ultra-violet") can "see" beyond the boundaries of human vision. It is much harder to grasp the concept of the space-time continuum, and to acknowledge the reality of planes of existence that we cannot (ordinarily, at least) perceive. Our three-dimensional world seems like all there is to the real world. The new physics says that's now quite unlikely. If time is a fourth dimension, how many more dimensions are unperceived realities? All this opens new doors for comprehending the possibility of life on a plane of existence beyond our present perceptive capabilities.

It is with considerable hesitation that I now go on to the frontiers of psychic matters. The whole field is so frought with pitfalls, rejection-on-principle in much of "the academy," the presence of poorly trained "researchers," and untrained "quacks." That has been well documented by *The Skeptical Inquirer*, for instance.[18] Some of the "academy" takes it seriously, however, such as Dr. Elizabeth Kubler-Ross. The experiences are here to stay and need to be studied with the same discipline and integrity that we apply in the more-accepted areas of investigation. Currently "parapsychology" has a status comparable to psychology's status before Freud. Some work has been done, but not much, relatively. I believe that the "academy" needs to admit it to its sacred halls, give it respectability, discipline it rigorously, and see what we can learn from it. That's a frontier for the future, and it may shed some light on what death really is, and what a human being really is. At this point, psychic phenomena seem to support the popular Orphic/Platonic dualistic view against the holistic view carried to its logical conclusion, but such conclusions are too tentative at the present time to be given the status of a serious projection into the future.

In summary, there will be circumstantial changes in our patterns of dying, in that we will more likely die at home than in the hospital. There will probably not be any change in the popular views of the cause(s) of "natural" death. We will probably continue to understand death itself in the ancient Orphic-Platonic sense of release of the soul (spirit, self) from the non-essential body, and we will probably learn some new things from the new physics and from psychic research data.

NOTES

1. Quoted from "Song of Nezhualcoyotl," a sixteenth-century Aztec poem. From Robert F. Weir, editor, *Death in Literature* (N.Y.: Columbia University Press, 1980), p. 18.
2. John Naisbitt, *Megatrends* (1982); Warner Books Edition (N.Y.: Warner Books, Inc., 1984), p. 153.
3. See Alvin Toffler, *The Third Wave*, first published by William Morrow in 1980, with several subsequent editions, all unchanged.
4. Ernest Becker, *The Denial of Death*, first published by the Free Press, a division of Macmillan Publishing Co., Inc., in 1973 and reissued in paperback in 1975.
5. Lucretius (c. 94-55 B.C.E.). "On the Nature of Things" (Rolfe Humphries, translator), as reprinted in Robert F. Weir, editor, *Death in Literature* (N.Y.: Columbia University Press, 1980), p. 10.
6. Isaiah 45:6-7, Revised Standard Version, with "Yahveh" replacing "The LORD."
7. *Ecclesiastes* 3:1-2, Revised Standard Version.
8. The original edition was published by G.P. Putnam's Sons in 1973, with many subsequent editions and printings, all unchanged.
9. *The Denial of Death* (First Free Press Paperback Edition, 1975), p. 283.
10. *The Quarterly Review*, Vol. 5, No. 4, p. 23.
11. *Ecclesiastes* 4:2. Revised Standard Version.
12. *Ecclesiastes* 7:1, Revised Standard Version.
13. *Ecclesiasticus*, or *The Wisdom of Jesus the Son of Sirach*, 41:1-2, Revised Standard Version.
14. This section is part of "The Carol of Death" sung by the "gray-brown bird" in section 14 of "When Lilacs Last in the Dooryard Bloomed," in Whitman's *Leaves of Grass* (many editions!). I have used the Signet Classic Edition, in the 1958 printing, where the quoted part appears on pp. 269-270.
15. *Ecclesiastes* 3:11, Revised Standard Version.
16. Page 26, paperback edition, 1975.
17. "On The Nature of Things," as found in Robert F. Wier, editor, *Death in Literature* (N.Y.: Columbia University Press, 1980), p. 17.
18. This is a periodical dedicated to expose all forms of "parapsychology," "extra-sensory perception," and "psychic" phenomena as unreal, "pseudo-science."

Death as a Factor
in Understanding Modern Attitudes
Toward the Aging:
A Symbolization-Avoidance Theory

W. Paul Jones, PhD

SUMMARY. This article challenges the adequacy of the eight primary theories that are used to analyze and account for what happens to persons in contemporary U.S. culture during the aging process. The theory presented in this article, Symbolization-Avoidance Theory, draws its clue from contrasting attitudes toward death during several periods in this country's history. The author suggests that there is a direct correlation between the modern avoidance/denial of death through "removal," and the image of elders as symbolic reminders of death, resulting in their rejection/departmentalization through "invisibility." This phenomenon, destined to become a growing dynamic in the future, is the dynamic known as "ageism."

David Stannard's *The Puritan Way of Death*[1] is an informative description of the tracing of the evolution of Western attitudes toward death from the Puritan Period to the present day. But more importantly, his study provides us with some clues that have led to the development of a *Symbolization-Avoidance Theory of Aging*, a theory that helps us understand the ever-increasing inclination toward a negative definition of the function of the elderly in our society.

W. Paul Jones is Professor of Philosophical Theology and Director of Doctoral Studies at Saint Paul School of Theology. He has a BA in literature from Mt. Union College (1954), a BD in Bible from Yale Divinity School, a MA in Philosophy from Yale University Graduate School, and a PhD in Philosophical Theology from Yale. He has taught at Yale and Princeton Universities.

The author wishes to thank Virginia Pych for her helpful comments on an earlier version of this article.

75

Stannard explores the contrasting manner in which children are socialized regarding death in different periods of American history. Puritan children, for example, were introduced to death as soon as possible; their spirituality required meditation upon the terrifying realities of metaphysical separation from God, for eternal damnation was always a possibility. In the Romantic Period that followed (19th century), children likewise were taught about death early and persistently. The motive here, however, was radically different — rather than bringing children to fear death, they were groomed to desire it. Death was understood as a glorious reunion, a birthing into eternity.

While these two approaches were diametrically opposed, there was agreement at one point: children should be introduced to death early so that they might become familiar with it, not only as an inevitable personal reality but as a significant factor for the focusing of life itself. By heavy contrast, however, in the 20th century there is almost total reversal of this attitude toward death that had operated without question for "new world" whites since the time of Plymouth Colony. The result has been the segregation of death from daily life, through a process entailing what Goldscheider calls "specialized bureaucracies."[2]

No doubt the contemporary lowering of child mortality rates among the non-poor has played a role in the statistical distancing of children from the reality of death. The lessening of childhood risk has encouraged a low profile for death, and extensive studies over the past half century confirm that "in large measure modern children have accepted their parent's frequent admonitions not to worry about it (death); since it is something that only afflicts the aged."[3] Schilder and Wechsler likewise allude to old age as the growing symbolic repository of a fear once spread throughout the age spectrum, beginning with early youth. Indicatively, for modern children

> one's own death is . . . either frankly neglected or it appears as such a distant event that one has not to worry about it. Old age, in the minds of most children, is like a far-off land, so remote that even speculation of ever reaching it appears as an idle, useless thought.[4]

This process of distancing leads to a non-reality of death that is based on "invisibility." Therefore, as Stannard observes, 20th-century children will grow into adulthood facing death not with a Puri-

tan encounter bordering on terror, nor with Romantic "sentimentali-
zation" and desire bordering on seduction. Rather the modern
approach is one of *avoidance and denial* through skillful and determined "social compartmentalization." E. S. Schneidman portrays
well the result of this rapid movement, in only one or two generations, toward the tremendous secularization of death: persons today
die "ascetically in antiseptic hospitals" rather than at home, drama-
tized by the physician who has replaced the priest, with mystery
residing in the medicine that has the power either to extend life or to
comfort our last gasps. And when it is over, the same process is
extended as the mortuary profession orchestrates the emotional
transition that cleanly disposes of death by pleasant removal.[5]

There is mounting evidence that in the transition from the 19th
century to the modern "ethos," death increasingly has become symbolic for an enveloping social process, one in which the "anonymity
and simple unimportance of the *individual* is made a working assumption in modern life, making it almost impossible for persons to
regard themselves or anyone else as truly unique and irreplace-
able."[7] That is, in the modern situation of *social* contingency, death
as *ontic* contingency becomes shaped with uncanny power. As symbol, death has become the ultimate reminder of our fragile and contingent status at each point in a social order built "invisibly" on
"expendableness" — throwaway resources that assume throwaway
workers. It is not strange, then, that such a dynamic forces death
and its reminding co-symbols, conscious and unconscious, into a
status and domain whereby the experience can be "prematurely"
avoided. The resultant fact is that today death is "socially unacceptable."

Consequently we are able to have a clearer understanding of the
fact that while most Americans die in hospitals or nursing homes,
this is *not* because of their need of specialized medical treatment.
Rather it results from two other dynamics: (1) There is a growing
and relentless "specializing" tendency to characterize aging as a
"fatal" and "terminal disease";[7] and (2) as this linking of death
with aging intensifies, an inevitable concomitant "conspiracy"
emerges that renders death's harbingers invisible. Increasingly *it is
the aged person who is seen as the primary herald or omen of
death*. Cooley's "looking glass self," eye to eye, skull to skull.

Last month one of my relatives sent his wife to a large clinic in a
major city 75 miles away. When she was diagnosed as "terminal,"
with nothing medically to be done, he chose with determined emo-

tion not to bring her home, but to place her in the hometown hospital. "I can't handle seeing her die," he explained. This story puts
faces to Stannard's report that it is common for hospital personnel to
avoid telling relatives the seriousness of a patient's illness, for fear
that the relatives will desert the patient. Ironic though the truth be, *it
is our own fear of death* that results in the often brutal isolation of
the very dying person whom we "love." Indeed, it is usually the
family who create for dying persons "a process marked by loneliness, irrelevance, and an absence of awareness."[8]

Our concern is to understand the dynamic that underlies this rapid
and intense reversal of attitudes toward death and the elderly. We
can begin to see that these attitudes are linked with the issue of
"ageism." In fact "dying" now functions for many persons as near-
identical image for "aging." Discern the meaning of contemporary
language and practice, as, for example, when a patient is medically
"introduced" into death through an induced comatose state, so as to
"reduce the emotionally threatening object – the dying patient – to a
socially non-functioning state prior to death. . . . "[9] This approach
creates a state of "premature social extinction," so that life for the
rest can go on.[10] If such an approach characterizes dying, it will
come almost inevitably to characterize our attitude toward the elderly as well. Notice that dying persons and the elderly are described very similarly: the "socially non-functioning" are dealt with
by "social compartmentalization" so as not to be "emotionally
threatening" by being placed in a state of "premature social extinction" whereby our "life can go on." Just as we are discouraged from
seeing dead persons until we are well into adulthood and seldom
experience the "dying process" of others, so too do we rarely see
the "aged" until required, and even more rarely, if at all, are we
"permitted" to experience their aging process. Stannard draws the
conclusion:

> Death has come to be viewed as an unwelcomed stranger
> rather than an expected companion, and many adults refuse to
> discuss it or even think about it. Their denial of death has
> extended to their children.

It is important for us here to see the correlate, drawn by Daniel
O'Hare that is following rapidly as conclusion: "Terminally ill persons are the twentieth century's Western lepers. We build a wall
around them and stand safely outside it."[11] And so it is inevitably

with the aged. For reasons integrally and symbolically related, there is a growing agreement among anthropologists such as Geoffrey Gorer, social historians such as Philippe Aries, and psychiatrists such as Robert Lifton and Eric Olson that society's perception of death is as a "disease" needing to be controlled by removal of its expressions, much as one attempts to isolate incurable illness, as if contagious.[12] And so even though (as Judith Stillion and Hannelore Wass remind us) prior to the 20th century children lived continuously with the fact of death from infancy through adulthood, a radical reversal is now occurring in which death becomes more distant at the same time that there is a rise in the phenomenon of "ageism." We are ready, then, to focus these beginning observations in terms of our Symbolization-Avoidance Theory of Aging.

One important issue that this theory addresses is the following critique offered by Kastenbaum and Aisenburg. They report that two out of every five adult depressive patients have lost at least one parent by age 15 (control groups were one out of every eight, and one out of every five).[13] The conclusion to be drawn from such statistics is that society's ambiguities about death are responsible for confusing young people as they attempt to make sense out of life in the face of death.[14] This vicious circle continues throughout life, becoming ominous, for in spite of extraordinary societal convolutions aimed at concealing death, when it does occur death only exacerbates what William May calls "an inner sense of bankruptcy before it." Is there any wonder, then, that so many today are feeling that there is "no alternative but to cling to life and avoid direct confrontation with the unknown"?[15] This one statement about the Western approach to death, we believe, is equally and relatedly a grounding statement for the present and future attitude toward the elderly.

And so we should not be surprised that we feel so "strange" and ill at ease in the "world" of the aged. In a society seemingly unable to succor us against deep feelings of loneliness, dispensability, and fragility of living, it follows inevitably that the elderly become symbols of myriad deaths to be avoided even in the mind. That is, our response to death results inevitably from our approach to life, and our response to both is "bewilderment and fear before the prospect of emptiness."[16] To complete the vicious circle, this threat of emptiness puts us into a conflict situation with those whom we commit to emptiness in order to render them invisible to us. (See Figure 1.)

This brings us to yet another irony. The result of our energetic

FIGURE 1

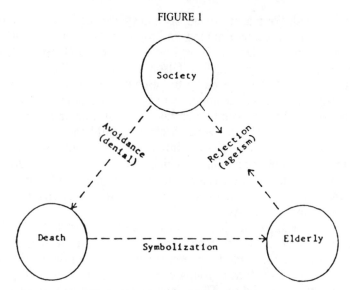

Symbolization-Avoidance Process

contrivance to avoid the awareness of death is the socializing of the elderly to see death as preferable to (or at least not significantly different from) their assigned invisibility. Even Elizabeth Kubler-Ross has been accused (by the *Wall Street Journal*!) of being part of the modern conspiracy to evade death by denial. In fact, her early fear of making death *too* appealing ("romantic") through her "findings" may help to identify a motivation for her recent interest in "death and dying."

Nevertheless, whenever most of us touch death today, we prefer to avoid it, or second best, remain "distanced" from it. Death happens only to *others*. And when *forced* to speak of death, the qualifiers of "if" or "may" or "perhaps" are employed to blunt even the facticity of death's relentless inevitability. We can understand, then, the research that shows that the greatest uneasiness over death is evidenced by the middle aged. That is, fear by the "spectators" (middle aged) exceeds that of the "participants" (the elderly), again increasing the alienation between the two groups, leading to even further "distancing." And the persistent distancing of the inevitable (death) results in a process of "false consciousness," which evokes the mutual pretense of those desiring not to imagine with those wishing not to remember.[17]

Recent explorations of the so-called mid-life crisis reveal one of the growing cracks in the complex attempt to achieve the deceptive social stability described above. This crisis marks the time when persons "confront their own mortality, finitude, limitations, their own death," beginning "to know in a very personal way that we are contingent, non-absolute beings. . . ."[18] We are expendable, merely temporary actors on the stage of social history. "The experience brings to the surface some feelings of dread."[19] Levinson's words are pointed: "Experience of one's mortality is at the core of the mid-life crisis."[20] Yet it is important that we understand that this crisis haunts all of us to some degree in at least isolated moments throughout life. Therefore the fundamental issue emerges not only with the sensed demise of our bodies, but it more broadly relates to the potential mortality of the very symbol structure of culture that promised the stability that is necessary for lived meaning. "Some preoccupation with death — fearing it, being drawn to it, seeking to transcend it — is not uncommon in all transitions. . . . "[21] Thus if the possibility of death is permitted to dawn in full strength, what stands to be exposed is "the mortality of . . . the myths by which we lived. The death of such myths creates a vacuum which anxiety intensifies."[22] No wonder death has become so socially unacceptable, for it evokes the pervasive fear "that nothing will last in the face of possible total destruction and that therefore nothing matters."[23] This is why death has become as much an unmentionable in our time as sex was in the Victorian era. "The natural processes of corruption and decay have become disgusting, as disgusting as the natural processes of birth and copulation were a century ago."[24] These are subjects fitting, in both cases, only for "pornography." Thus our literature stands in stark contrast to literature of previous periods, so much so that Gorer could not recall a single novel or play in the last 20 years that has a "deathbed" scene in it.

Leo Tolstoy's story, *The Death of Ivan Ilych*, captures the heart of the dynamic we are exploring:

> What tormented Ivan Ilych most was the deception, the lie, which *for some reason they all accepted*, that he was not dying but was simply ill . . . their not wishing to admit what they all knew . . . wishing and forcing him to participate in that lie . . . destined to degrade this awful, solemn act to the level of their visitings, their curtains, their sturgeon for dinner. . . . The awful, terrible act of his dying was, he could see,

reduced by those about him to the level of a casual, unpleas-
ant, and almost indecorous incident. . . . This falsity around
him and within him did more than anything else to poison his
last days.[25]

Simone de Beauvoir, wrestling with the death of her mother in the
face of her previous assumption of death as "natural," expresses an
important new voice against society's denial. *Death is enemy*, an
"unjustifiable violation" that always comes too soon or too late,
violently or corrosively, in which one always dies "from something" that rips and tears "the reassuring curtain of everyday trivial-
ity" so as to call one's world into "radical question."[26] Recognizing
such a symbolic threat, certain researchers of the mid-life crisis are
beginning to suggest the very conclusion we have been drawing:
"People don't want the elderly around to remind them of their finitude. There is a centrifugal force at work, hurling older people to
the circumference of life."[27]

We believe that our Symbolization-Avoidance Theory has important implications for understanding modern and future relations between children and the aged. While Puritan children might fear the
aged as harbinger of their own eventual terror, there was nonetheless
a deep seriousness in the relation — a seriousness that emerged from
a profound curiosity that was carved out of a mutually bonding mystery. The Puritan family gathered around the deathbed, welded together in what seemed to function "liturgically" as a cosmic drama.
Many are the powerful accounts written by Puritan offspring recall-
ing their spiritual experiences through the death-experience of the
aged. Later, in the Romantic period, the attitude of children toward
the aged became more imaginative, sparked by a fascination
whereby children experienced even a physical beauty in the whole
process. What stark constrast, then, is to be seen in the anti-relation
between modern children and the aged. At best the relationship
tends to be reduced to carefully scheduled visits, preceded by a
rehearsal of "good behavior," with the "back stage self" of each
and all being groomed avoidance.

Many current attempts to break down this avoidance fail because
they only treat the symptoms. Strategies for racial integration are
illustrative. For example, during 1967-81 efforts by certain whites
in Kansas City to reduce racial tension led to the idea of integrated
"Dinners for Ten." Evaluations of this extended monthly exposure
of racially diverse couples indicated that at best attitudinal change

was not toward "race" but toward select individuals. Typical "enlightened" comments were: "I really came to like Elsie; she's not
like the others." Or, "If the rest were like Joe, there wouldn't be a
problem." The same process, we offer, is true of exposure with the
aged. The "am," which Irving Goffman has described well in other
settings, is here that of a grandfather who must be seen as "spry"
for his age. He is one who "likes to play our kind of games." "I'm
pleased by how happy he is — I like his smile." When the drama of
avoidance is over, grandfather has lost by winning, or won by losing. His offspring image him as "like them," just an older "adult."
And any guilt for him being in the nursing home is assuaged because "he really is happy there." Meanwhile, grandfather remains
invisibly alienated in his back stage self, isolated by the image-lie in
which he participated, of being "the exception," rendering him unknown and profoundly alone. And he, in turn, with growing pain
comes to measure himself against this dramaturgical model — a
model that is attainable with increasing difficulty only for special
front stage occasions. Death comes to be preferable.

* * * *

At least eight theories have been developed to describe what happens to persons as they age. A short summary of each of these
theories will help in understanding better the unique contribution of
the Symbolization-Avoidance Theory that we are proposing. [28]

1. *Continuity Theory.* [29] This theory rests on the optimistic insistence that change, growth, and development continue throughout
the human life span and are not limited to the social, psychological,
and physiological changes generally associated with old age. Therefore there is no more homogeneity among the aging than there is
among any other age group. The effect is to render the aged invisible as a distinct group. Our theory agrees here, but for different
reasons; we believe this invisibility is a social intentionality.

2. *Role Theory.* [30] According to Role Theory, two types of
changes occur in the aging process: the relinquishment of "adult"
relationships and roles, and the acceptance of new roles that are
characteristic of the retirement stage. While descriptively accurate,
this theory is hardly useful in accounting for the "why" of such
obvious transition.

3. *Activity Theory.* [31] Havighurst expanded on "role theory" by
linking it to "life satisfaction" through activity. The greater the role,

the more actively involved persons become; the smaller the role, the less the activity. And the reverse is also operative — as activity decreases with age, these persons' roles become smaller. Although this theory is usually stated positively, Symbolization-Avoidance Theory suggests that the elimination of essential role is linked with avoidance, whereby the only activity that results is variation on the theme of "time consumption." One study concluded that it is only social activity with friends that relates significantly to life satisfaction for elders.[32] This may suggest the need for an "elder" subculture in which alternative values can arise through honest refusal at avoidance games, outwardly and inwardly.[33]

4. *Socioenvironmental Theory.*[34] Jaben F. Gubrium, wishing to account for the apparent exceptions to the Activity and Disengagement Theories (discussed below), expanded the category of "activity" to include not only social expectations but individual ones as well, making for greater pluralism in the aging dynamic. This expansion seems descriptively accurate.

5. *Subculture Theory.*[35] By pulling together insights from the last several theories, one can postulate the actual existence of a subculture of aging, for subcultures occur whenever individuals of any segment of the population (1) interact with each other more than others; and/or (2) experience exclusion from the general population. This theory identifies both factors as present for the aged in contemporary culture. The arbitrary Social Security age of 65 has produced a threshold, in which one is pushed to perceive oneself as "progressively physically and mentally handicapped," therefore evoking a movement "from independent to dependent, and from aspiring to declining."[36]

Subculture Theory is an application of the social theory known as Symbolic-Interactionism and is helpful in perceiving both the fact of exclusion and the creative possibilities of compensatory value formation that are possible when our society forces the aged close together. Yet it neglects the contention of Continuity Theory that pluralism within the aging population is centrifugal to such formation. Thus if such a subculture is to be significant, elders need to become conscious of exclusion as intentional and structured — letting the sense of exclusion arouse feelings that are sufficiently aggressive to generate conflict with the rest of society. Although Subculture Theory tends to be too optimistic about the mental attitude and the opportunity situation of the aging for acting out an alternative behavior, it is helpful in recognizing (as many theories do not) that the "disengagement" of the aged from society is *neither voluntary nor desired*.

6. *Disengagement Theory.*[37] The weight of the previous theories moves us toward a serious consideration of the disengagement view. Built upon a structural functionalist sociological analysis combining shades of Durkheim and Parsons, this theory holds that "successful aging" is a socialized process of mutual social and psychological disengagement acted out jointly by society and the individual for the sake of stable social functioning. In effect, one becomes socialized to die for the sake of incorporating younger members into the process of social continuity. It is strange how widespread the acceptance of this theory has been. It is a kind of socialized holocaust, in which the person who is no longer able to make positive contributions to the society is expected to withdraw from it. The rationale for such disengagement is to fit younger people into the system by enabling society sufficient distance from the dying process for optimum living to occur. We can sense precisely here evidence of the "avoidance" dynamic that was discussed earlier. Yet rather than holding a positive view of disengagement, as this view does, we are contending a negative one. It is our position that modern U.S. society desires disengagement from the aged because the aged represent *symbolic confrontation*: (a) with our *social expendability*, an expendability that is theoretically recognized but distanced; and (b) with our *metaphysical expendability*, which is deeply repressed by departmentalization. It is a disengagement of avoidance, not a disengagement of healthy functioning.

Our position is confirmed by Dumont's and Foss' study showing that Americans intellectually acknowledge death, while on the unconscious feeling level we deny it with feverish obstinacy.[38] It is of deep significance that we hide and disguise not only corpses but our own feelings and questions. In fact, even direct language statements about death and dying are regarded as crude, to be replaced by euphemisms. And so, we are compelled to conclude this: *Disengagement focused on death and its symbols is a life stance which in being acted out finds expression as ageism.*

It is ironic that the traditional positive Disengagement Theory rests on a sociological theory that heralds the stabilizing function of religion. That is, aged persons view self-negation as a duty within the religio-social claims identified by Durkheim. Yet, ironically, the very society that seemingly requires such religious sanctions is precisely the society that, according to David O. Moberg, undercuts religion for related reasons. The current decline of religion can be traced directly to "declining mortality rates and to the concentration of death among the elderly who already have been removed from the center of family life and the workaday world." [39]

That is, the removal of death from life's center undercuts the power of the religious to sustain that very social stability that depends upon a religiously-based self-negation by elders. It is revealing that Elaine Cumming, in explicating her Disengagement Theory, admits that the theory "does not concern itself with the effects of the great scourges of old age, poverty, and illness." [40] Precisely.

7. *Social Breakdown Theory.* [41] We move closer to the possibility of putting these various theories together into a whole by looking at the work of Kuypers and Bengston. Returning to the symbolic interactionist perspective, Social Breakdown Theory holds that social conditions such as loss of role and of reference group rob elders of *feedback* in self-definition and validation. This feedback vacuum communicates to elders that they are "obsolete" and "useless." And such socio-environmental change creates a pathological quality in the aged, in which, one might assume, death *does* then become positive by contrast. In the context of this theory the seemingly positive socialization process reflected in the disengagement view has at best the questionable status of a double negative: the aged accept death because it is a better negation than societal negation. A positive contribution of Social Breakdown Theory, however, is that the "false consciousness" of the aged is identified. Yet, like the other theories, the "why" of such breakdown has not been identified and explored.

8. *Age Stratification.* [42] Resting on a conflict model of social theory, this position uses the concepts of social class (inequality of income, prestige, and power) and social mobility (movement between classes) to understand aging. Put another way, just as a Marxist perspective analyzes society in terms of class, this theory analyzes society according to age. Age is a dynamic, organic, inescapable factor throughout society. The importance of this accentuation of age permeation for the Symbolization-Avoidance Theory is the implication that the symbolic function of the aged operates according to self-interest throughout the whole social fabric. Accordingly, each age structure affects both attitudes and behavior. This view, however, remains largely descriptive, with little attention to cause.

9. *Symbolization-Avoidance Theory.* Basically this theory, as

proposed by us, attempts to explicate the *cause* of disengagement, which goes unexplored in most of the other theories. Once the cause is identified, we believe that it will be possible to incorporate dimensions of these other theories into an organic whole.

Symbolization-Avoidance Theory finds its clue for understanding the function of aging in future U.S. culture through the present attitude toward death. As illustrated earlier, there seems to be a direct correlation between our current avoidance/denial of death through "removal" and the image of elders as symbols of death, resulting in the rejection/departmentalization through "invisibility" as ageism. "Death," as it functions in this dynamic, symbolizes contingency in varied forms, ranging from social expendability through personal unacceptability to final ontic fragility. The inability to deal creatively with death on the part of this culture has as its result the ethos that becomes structured as ageism.

We draw on symbolic interactionism to understand the process by which the elder comes to changed self-identity, effected as part of the stabilization dynamics of society well understood by structural functionalists. The result is well described as a conflict understanding (unconscious or conscious) of the relation of the aged to the rest of society. Expressed another way, avoidance is groomed economically, while rooted essentially in metaphysical causes. The aged thereby become symbolic repository of anxiety, rendering a negative version of the Disengagement Theory.

From this base, Symbolization-Avoidance Theory can dialogue with other theories. It agrees with Continuity Theory, but identifies the lack of homogeneity among the aging as expression of the thoroughness of the socializing process of a society who needs to erase the focusing presence (rather than as evidence of the absence of an alienated class). The point of agreement with Role Theory is that retirement does entail significant role change; with Activity Theory there is agreement that reduced productive role does indeed tend to result in lessened activity. And building upon Socioenvironmental Theory, we perceive that significant "life satisfaction" for elders in contemporary societal life would necessitate a conscious development of an individual meaning expectation that is in clear tension with the socialization from societal expectations. Encouragement of alternative values could occur, according to Subculture Theory, when awareness of intentional exclusion escalates into a self-interested interaction of the aging as a group. We can see, then, that Symbolization-Avoidance Theory provides the *cause* of the disengagement between the aged and the rest of society, giving focus for the descriptive insights of other theories.

Thus societal equilibrium is protected through diminution of a menacing contingency, symbolized by the aging as threat, requiring that elders be so socialized that they "will" invisibility, at best as "duty," and at worst in accordance with Social Breakdown Theory, i.e., being socialized into obsolete uselessness, so that even in their own eyes, death is no longer to be feared but accepted as preferable to social isolation. Such "logic" can identify with Age Stratification Theory, for the conflict dynamic characteristic of class analysis parallels that implied by age analysis. In spite of our sentiments to the contrary, the truth is that for our culture the aged are foe. At best, we have patronization as a method of neutralization. At its normal worst, we have the image of "death trajectory," institutionalizing as schedule the dying process itself, programming as part the elderly as "walking dead."

Sociologist David O. Moberg detects something of this correlation that emerges from our theory. Thanatophobia, he states, contributes to gerontophobia, the prejudicial attitude behind the discriminatory practices of ageism.[43] Simone de Beauvoir draws clearly the implication, if resolution of ageism is to be possible. To change our attitude toward the aged entails a change of our attitude toward life. Put another way, ageism, in the end, is a deeply theological issue:

> To overcome ageism, we must overcome the taboo on death. . . . The meaning of death is a central religious question. The largely unconscious attempt to avoid it is a deeply spiritual phenomenon.[44]

Indeed, the solution to ageism that deals with cause rather than symptom will finally be "religious." In a real sense ageism is a deep struggle within all of us that attempts to avoid the religious question. But "religious" need not imply *any* answer: at this point it need only imply the willingness not to negate the *question*. Whitehead expressed this same conclusion more completely: "Apart from the religious vision, human life is a flash of occasional enjoyment lighting up a mass of pain and misery, a bagetelle of transient experience."[45] It follows in the foreseeable future that without such vision, "Elderly, get thou behindst me."

NOTES

1. David Stannard, *The Puritan Way of Death* (New York: Oxford, 1977).
2. Calvin Goldscheider, "The Social Inequality of Death." In E. S. Schneidman, *Death: Current Perspectives* (Palo Alto: Mayfield, 1976), pp. 118-23.
3. Stannard, *The Puritan Way of Death*, p. 189.
4. "The Attitudes of Children Towards Death," *Journal of Genetic Psychology*, 45 (1934), 421. Cf. Sylvia Anthony, *The Discovery of Death in Childhood and After* (London: Allen Lane, 1971). Noted by Stannard, p. 229.
5. E. S. Schneidman, *Death* . . . , pp. 10, 87, 124.
6. Stannard, *The Puritan Way of Death*, p. 190 (italics mine).
7. See Edman S. Schneidman, "Some Aspects of Psychotherapy with Dying Persons" in E. S. Schneidman, *Death* . . . , p. 206.
8. Stannard, p. 191 – includes statistics.
9. *Ibid.*, p. 192.
10. *Ibid.*, p. 193.
11. Daniel G. O'Hare, "The Experience of Dying." In Gari Lesnoff-Caravaglia (ed.), *Aging and the Human Condition* (New York: Human Sciences Press, 1982).
12. See Schneidman, *Death* . . . , p. 47c, 52f, 56f.
13. Robert Kastenbaum & Ruth Aisenberg, *The Psychology of Death* (New York: Springer, 1976) p. 1.
14. *Ibid.*, p. 15.
15. Stannard, *The Puritan Way of Death*, p. 194.
16. *Ibid.*
17. See Barney G. Glaser & Anselm L. Strauss, "The Ritual Drama of Mutual Pretense," in Schneidman, *Death* . . . , pp. 161-71.
18. Eugene Bianchi, "Aging as a Spiritual Journey," *JSAC Grapevine*, 15, (Nov. 1983), 1-2.
19. *Ibid.*
20. Daniel J. Levinson, et al., *The Seasons of a Man's Life* (New York: Alfred A. Knopf, 1978), p. 26.
21. *Ibid.*, p. 51.
22. Bianchi, p. 2.
23. Schneidman, *Death* . . . , p. 47.
24. Geoffrey Gorer, "The Pornography of Death." In Schneidman, *Death* . . . , p. 50.
25. Leo Tolstoy, *The Death of Ivan Ilych and Other Stories* (New York: Signet, 1960), pp. 137-8.
26. Simone de Beauvoir, "Epilogue to a Very Easy Death" in Schneidman, *Death* . . . , pp. 370-2.
27. Bianchi, "Aging . . . ," p. 2.
28. I am particularly dependent here upon Cary Kant and Barbara Manard (ed.), *Aging in America* (New York: Alfred, 1976), and upon Dr. David Oliver (Saint Paul School of Theology) for guidance with material in this field.
29. Richard H. Williams & Claudine G. Wirths, *Lives Through the Years* (New York: Atherton Press, 1965).
30. Leonard S. Cottrell, Jr., "The Adjustment of the Individual to His Age and Sex Roles," *American Sociological Review*, 7(Oct. 1942), 617-20. *Personal Adjustment in Old Age* (Chicago: Science Research Associates, 1949), pp. 6-7. (Ruth Cavan, Ernest Burgess, Robert Havighurst, Herbert Holdhame). Bernard S. Phillips, "A Role Theory Approach to Adjustment in Old Age." In Kant & Manard, *Aging* . . . , pp. 7-18.
31. Developed by Havighurst in the early 1950s.

32. Bruce W. Lemon, Vern L. Bengston, and James A. Peterson. "An Exploration of the Activity Theory of Aging: Activity Types and Life Satisfaction Among In-Movers to a Retirement Community," *Journal on Gerontology*, 27 (1972), 511-23. Albrecht, *Older Persons* (New York: Longmans, Green, 1953).

33. W. Paul Jones, "Aging as a Spiritualizing Process." In *Journal of Religion and Aging*, *1*, 1 (Fall 1984), pp. 3-16.

34. Jaber G. Gubrium, "Toward a Socio-Environmental Theory of Aging," *Gerontologist*, *12*, 281-4.

35. Arnold M. Rose, "The Subculture of the Aging: A Framework for Research in Social Gerontology." In A. M. Rose & W. Peterson, *Older People and Their Social Worlds* (Philadelphia: Davis, 1965), pp. 3-16. Arnold M. Rose, "The Subculture of the Aging: A Framework for Research in Social Gerontology," in Kant & Manard, *Aging . . .* , pp. 42-60.

36. Cary Kant & Barbara Manard, *Aging in America*, p. 53.

37. Elaine Cumming, Lois R. Dean, and David S. Newell. "Disengagement, a Tentative Theory of Aging," *Sociometry*, *23*, 1 (Mar. 1960); and E. C. & William E. Henry, *Growing Old* (New York: Basic Books, 1961). Elaine Cumming, "Further Thoughts on the Theory of Disengagement" in Kant & Manard, *Aging . . .* , pp. 19-41.

38. R. G. Dumont & D. C. Foss. *The American View of Death: Acceptance or Denial?* (Cambridge: Schenkman, 1972).

39. David O. Mobert. "Spiritual Well-Being of the Dying" in Gari Lesnoff-Caravaglia (ed.) *Aging and the Human Condition* (New York: Human Sciences Press, 1982), p. 140.

40. Cary Kant & Barbara Manard, *Aging in America*, p. 20.

41. Kuypers & Bengston.

42. Matilda White Riley. "Social Gerontology and the Age Stratification of Society," *Gerontologist*, *II* (1971), 79-87.

43. David O. Moberg, "Spiritual Well-Being of the Dying," p. 148.

44. *Ibid.*

45. Quoted by Bianchi, *Ibid.*

Research in Religion and Aging: An Unlikely Scenario

Earl D. C. Brewer, PhD

SUMMARY. Here is a brief review of the literature in religion and aging. It is followed by a theoretical framework within which various research questions are suggested. The "unlikely scenario" about future research work interrelating religion and aging perhaps calls for more significant interventions in terms of scholars and dollars than will be forthcoming. Only time will tell.

This scenario follows a tri-window approach.[1] The past is reviewed through the left window, the present is viewed through the middle window, and the future is previewed through the window on the right. Since the research and writings of the past exist in the present, these two windows may be joined in a brief literature review. The main constructive works here will be previewing possibilities through the third window.

REVIEWING AND VIEWING PAST AND PRESENT LITERATURE

In spite of its recognized importance in the lives of the elderly, little systematic research has been done in religion and aging. There are several reasons for this state of affairs. First and foremost is the effort to hybridize two major fields of study. Such cross-field or

Earl D. C. Brewer is Charles Howard Candler Professor Emeritus of Sociology and Religion, Candler School of Theology, Emory University, Atlanta, Georgia 30322. He is Adjunct Professor, The Gerontology Center, Georgia State University, Atlanta, Georgia 30303.

inter-disciplinary work is always difficult. Here it is unusually the case because studies in both religion and aging bring together many disciplines. Efforts to interrelate them theoretically and practically give rise to various problems. A theoretical/theological frame for research in this field is poorly focused with its outer edges even less well-defined. Exciting theoretical and applied possibilities lie ahead.

Second, government sources of funding for research in religion are almost nonexistent. This means that researchers in gerontology and related fields give little attention to religion. At best, the topic is a "piggy back" minor element in larger studies.

Third, religious organizations have only recently become responsive to the programmatic needs of the elderly in their congregations. This has resulted in policy statements, program manuals, and similar work. Few significant research projects have been supported either by individual denominations or by ecumenical organizations.

An exception has been the work of the National Interfaith Coalition on Aging. It brought together religious leaders and scholars in aging studies and applications. It did pioneering work in impacting theological education with gerontology.[2] An ecumenical organization, it received funds from the Office of Aging for this project. It continues to exert influence in the field of religion and aging.

The appearance of the *Journal of Religion & Aging* in the Fall of 1984 marked a step forward in scholarly work in the field. The first four issues contained 24 articles.[3] Although these could be classified in various ways, the following provides rough themes and numbers of articles: Spiritual — 3; Psychological — 2; Historical, Biographical — 4; Practice — 4; Research — 1; Theological Education — 2; Philosophical, Ethical, Theological — 4; and Religious Organizations — 4. The research relied heavily on the descriptive, historical, and ethical methods. There was little evidence of empirical research using either social or physical science methodology. Interestingly, most of the books reviewed in these issues did not deal directly with the religious involvement in aging. Perhaps this was an indication of the paucity of book-length works in the field.

A bench-mark annotated bibliography[4] showed 504 references. Most of them were articles, chapters or booklets. The materials were grouped under three broad headings: The Religion of the Elderly — 114 items, Organized Religion in the Service of the Elderly — 125, Spiritual Ministration to the Elderly — 109, and Miscellaneous — 125. In addition, there were 31 titles without annotation.

A more recent bibliography⁵ naturally contained many of the references found in the Fecher work. It also listed more recent articles, chapters, pamphlets and, especially, books. Both bibliographies seem to show more scholarly articles in gerontological than religious journals.

This latter bibliography was prepared for the 1986 annual meeting of the American Society on Aging (formerly the Western Gerontological Society). In cooperation with the National Interfaith Coalition on Aging, the Society sponsored a special program on Religion, Spirituality, and Aging. It also featured a Religion and Aging Track as part of its regular program.

This brief review of the literature interrelating studies in religion and aging indicates that there is growing interest and energy in this hybrid area of endeavor. It is now time to fantasize about future possibilities.

PREVIEWING – AN UNLIKELY SCENARIO

The scenes through the window of the future may range as widely as capacities to imagine. The most likely picture of the future is a continuation of the past and present, as seen above. That is, unless some significant interventions occur. Among these could be efforts to conceptualize theoretical/theological approaches within which research questions could be raised and quests mounted to search for answers. A modest effort along these lines is intended here.

Obviously, any attempt to develop a model interlacing the many disciplines converging on the fields of religion and aging is fraught with hazards. Also, such an effort will be greatly influenced by one's own perspective or location in the scheme of things. Thus, if this model smacks of the social sciences, especially sociology, do not be surprised.⁶ Perhaps it may stimulate those in other disciplines to go and do likewise.

This model is based on the assumption that relations and symbolic interactions are fundamental in human behavior.⁷ The metaphor of weaving may be appropriate to aid in visualizing human relations. Diagram 1 shows a circular "loom." *I/We* are seen in the center. *I* designates the subjective aspect of the self and *We* of the group. Human weaving is done by the person or the group as relations develop and as time passes. The "loom" is divided into four types of relationships or strands for weaving. The *I-Me* relations go

DIAGRAM 1

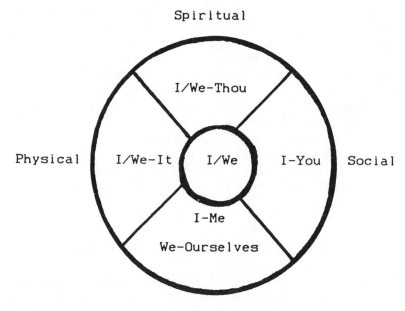

on inside the individual. *I* is seen as the center of consciousness together with all that *I* am conscious of. *Me* is the objective aspect of the self and is the most intimate relation of *I*. *I-Me* relations go on within the inner experiences and memories of the self. When two or more selves join in relations, *We* emerges. *We-Ourselves* denotes the intragroup pluralization of *I-Me* relations. These relations are shown at the base of the "loom" and are essential to all other weaving. *I* and *We* are the weavers as well as the woven.

Moving around the circle to the left, we encounter the *It* relations. These concern the human body and the total physical environment. This includes food, clothing, and shelter as well as all natural and human-made physical entities. *I/We-It* strands weave humans into the whole fabric of physical life.

On the other side of the "loom" are the *You* relations. *I-You* may be simple one-on-one dyads or complex *We-Them* organizational relations. Here fall in place the major institutions and organizations of a society, such as marriage and family, schools and education, recreation and arts, politics and government, economics and jobs, religion and churches.

At the top of the circle is the *I/We-Thou* spiritual relationships. The *Thou* of this relation may result from over-beliefs, to use William James'[8] phrase, and other intensive experiences. *I/We-Thou* relations may be characterized as holy, deeply emotional, wholistic, with unusual commitments. *Thou* partakes of the transcendent, the mysterious, the eternal, the infinite, and so on. It pushes the human spirit to its farthest reaches, toward a sense of destiny and ultimacy. Different names for gods and spirits have been attached to this relation in different societies. Ethically and historically, some of the lowest and blackest, as well as some of the highest and brightest moments of human behavior have flowed out of the *I/We-Thou* relations.

Obviously, the actual use of these relations as strands for weaving aspects of everyday life would envision them as intertwining. Each type of relation would go out from the center (I/We) toward the circumference and return. It would also move around the circle to form intermingled strands in the tapestries of life.

Although internally dynamic, the relational picture of Diagram 1 needs to be supplemented by a temporal dimension. This is displayed in Diagram 2. The "arrow of time" is shown along the life line from birth to death. This is divided into four broad units of childhood, youthhood, adulthood and elderhood. Calibration into rough groups of years is possible but unimportant here. The "loom" of Diagram 1 is located at the beginning of elderhood. This "loom" is overlaid with temporal and ethical dimensions. The center of the circle represents the present with memories of the past and anticipations of the future. This horizontal temporal transcendence supplements the bottom line birth-death chronology. In addition, the vertical lines represent ethical considerations of light and dark, health and sickness, good and bad, ascendence and descendence.

This presentation of a relational framework is much too brief. Yet perhaps it will serve to raise research questions in need of exploration. In any case, the task now is to go back over these elements and to suggest some needed research in religion and aging.

Perhaps the greatest research question for religion and aging grows out of the top of the circle in Diagram 1. What is the nature of the spiritual relation and how is it related to other dimensions of life? Modern human sciences tend to ignore the spiritual as nonexistent or nonessential. Religious studies focus primarily on the par-

DIAGRAM 2

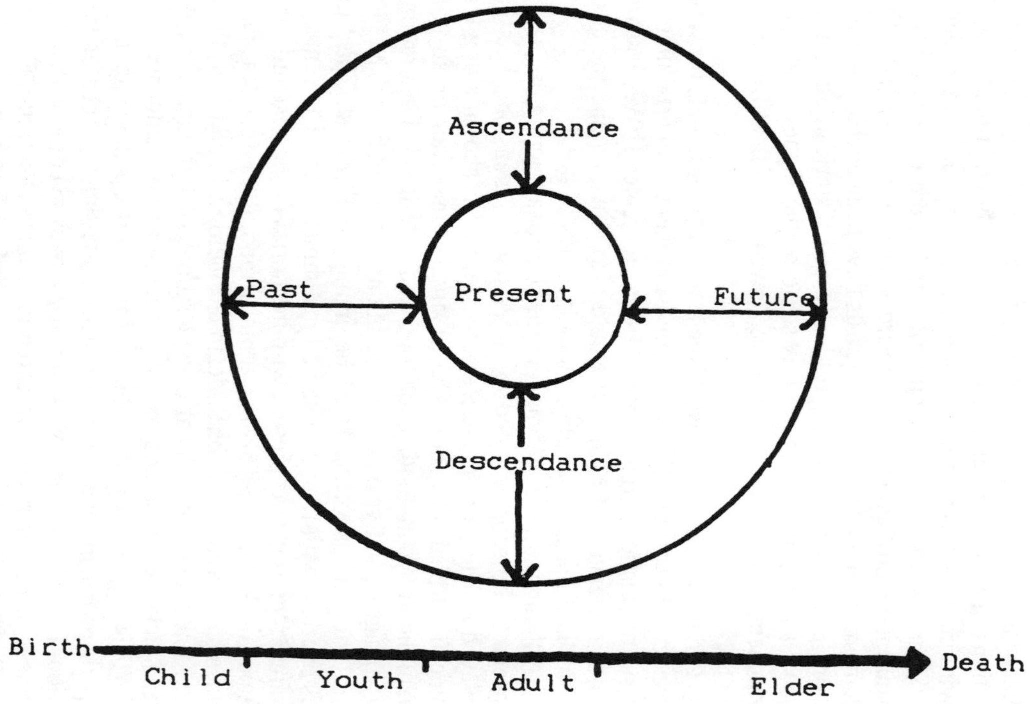

Ascendance

Present

Descendance

Future

Past

Birth — Child — Youth — Adult — Elder — Death

ticularities of their own traditions in terms of doctrines, organizational structures, and practices. The result is that spirituality is little explored, especially in modern western religions.

What is the spiritual dimension of human behavior? Is it the same as consciousness? Does it emerge out of the capacities of persons and groups to transcend themselves temporally (review the past and preview the future), spatially (think of other places while in this place), or ethically (reach for a higher goal or fall to a lower evil)? Is this spiritual relation found in all societies? Is it the natural effervescence flowing out of personal reflection and group interactions? [9] Are prayer and meditation the practical expressions of spirituality? What others? Can spirituality be taught and learned? Is there spiritual development and stages of growth? Can spirits soar as bodies decline? As social losses occur? As psychic and physical pain increases? What changes in spirituality occur among the elderly? Are spiritual relations likely to be different in different age cohorts? Do the elderly have opportunities for special development in spirituality? How is spirituality related to organized religion? How do congregations function to stimulate and guide spiritual development in the elderly in their membership and in the community? Is it possible to conceptualize spiritual well-being as parallel to mental and physical well-being? How are spiritual relations involved in physical, personal, and group relations? How do these impinge on the role of the elderly and their care givers? Other such research questions could be generated by mentally playing with the interrelations of Diagrams 1 and 2.

A second major area of research questions focuses on the *I/We-You/Them* relations, especially on organized religion. It is often assumed that religious organizations are designed to care for the spirits or souls of people. To what extent do congregations and other religious groups deal with the spiritual needs of the elderly? How are they related to their economic and physical needs (food, clothing, shelter, etc.), especially of the poor elderly? How do they deal with the social and psychological needs (companionship, self-esteem, continued learning and growth, etc.)? What policy statements and practices are developed and followed by major denominations? How are these implemented at the congregational level? Are theological schools equipping ministers to work with the elderly in their congregations? Is continuing education for clergy and laity available in this field? Are volunteers in congregations encouraged to work with programs and agencies dealing with the day-to-day needs of the elderly? What is the role of retired ministers? What provisions do denominations make for them? What about retired teachers, researchers and professionals who work with the elderly? What opportunities do they have in their retirement years?

How is religion involved in the values of the elderly? What strains and stresses in values and moral standards face older persons in view of the changes in lifestyles in the past few decades? For example, the traditional role of women and the new feminism; greater racial inclusiveness; freer sexual standards; relationships with adult children and grandchildren; increased leisure time; fear of aging, diseases (such as Alzheimers), and death? Changing moral standards and ethics involving life and death issues for the elderly and all age groups should be promising areas for research.

What are the roles of other major institutions in quality aging, such as family, government, business, schools? How do the various elements in the programs of congregations take into account the special needs of older persons? Examples: barrier free and special aids in the church building, liturgy, sermon, educational work, fellowship activities, home visits and pastoral care, death education and rituals. To what extent do the elderly have opportunities to be in volunteer service to and through congregations? How do congregations provide for intergenerational experience involving children, youth, adults and the elderly?

How are denominations involved in providing creative housing, medical care, economic assistance and other needs of older persons? How are those efforts related to secular service agencies for the elderly? How can the resources of religious organizations and other institutions be joined to work toward quality aging for all citizens?

Such questions dealing directly with spirituality and organized religion could be extended world without end. However, there are other lines of inquiry exposed by the diagrams. Extensive studies of aging have gone on in other quadrants of Diagram 1: psychological (*I-Me* relations),[10] social scientific (*I-You/We-Them* relations),[11] and biological (*I/We-It* relations).[12] Usually these are focused inquiries within the specific disciplines. It is clear from the theoretical model represented by the diagrams that everything is connected to everything else. Thus, there should be a call for such specialized studies to be related to the totality of the experiences of older persons, including the spiritual and religious aspects. This should require multidisciplinary team research in aging with full participation of religious scholars. Such research efforts would naturally flow into much needed multi-professional programs for the care of the elderly. Calls for wholistic interdisciplinary studies often fall on deaf ears in our highly specialized academic research and professional practice. This narrowcasting of research and practice may be important to continue only as it contributes to the broadcasting of understanding and ministry to the whole elderly individual or group.

In looking over the diagrams, what motifs or metaphors are likely to guide aging studies during the next generation of scholars? Will the physical relation continue to provide the major motif? What about the economic metaphor around housing, income, and other such needs? What about the well-off elderly and the poor elderly? Will the political power theme come to the fore? Will the search for the spiritual quality of life become significant? Will the artistic motif become important? What about leisure and recreation? Will the sense of a human journey from birth to death with review of the past and preview of the future become dominant? What opportunities for achievement and quality life for the elderly will be available through various aspects of our culture and society, especially through researchers and care givers?

What new human organizations or programs may need to be generated to meet the changing needs of the elderly, especially those in the 80's and above? Current examples are hospice and elderhostel.

These "stream of consciousness" questions could go on and on. The interrelations between the various strands and elements of the diagrams have hardly been treated. Other questions may touch the theoretical interests or the practical needs of some gerontologists and religious scholars. Research designs could be devised to explore answers. In the past this has largely been accomplished on an individual and ad hoc basis. Since the high points of the research and program activities of the National Interfaith Coalition on Aging and the recent efforts of the American Association of Retired Persons to impact theological education with gerontological material, little work on a systematic basis has been done. Only limited, if any, support from governmental sources may be anticipated. Informally, interested individuals from a wide range of backgrounds in gerontology and religion could keep in mind the role and status of the elderly in their own research and programs. For examples, biblical scholars could deal with the place of older persons in the Bible, and gerontologists could be concerned to research the relationship between aging agencies and congregations as care givers. Articles and research reports could find their ways into the usual journals of such scholars.

A more systematic approach to research in religion and aging would be to organize a section in the Gerontological Society of America or an independent religion and aging association. Research papers could be shared at annual meetings. Perhaps the *Journal of Religion & Aging* could become the official journal of such a group. In addition, centers for religion and aging studies might be sponsored. Details of such proposals would need careful attention, especially the interdisciplinary aspects.

It is evident that there is growing interest and activity in research dealing with religion and older persons.[13] Much more needs to be done to face the increase in the numbers and the longevity of the elderly in the 21st century.

Theological schools as intellectual centers of organized religion have a special reponsibility in the areas of theoretical/theological and applied research in this field. This is obviously extended to teaching in the practice of ministries to, with, for and by the elderly. This might involve teams of scholars from different theological disciplines together with researchers from the fields related to gerontology.

It is fantasized here that seminaries and denominational leaders will increasingly become aware of the significance of this field for research and practice. This will be followed, so the fantasy goes, by appropriate commitments of scholars and dollars to this enterprise.

This scenario of some urgent research questions interrelating religion and aging and possibilities for dealing with them may seem unrealistic and unlikely to be the direction of the future. Perhaps theoretical/theological developments and practical experiences in team research will come in other ways. It appears that leadership and interest point to breakthroughs in this area. Certainly, the impact of increased numbers as "baby-boomers" join the ranks of older persons during the next few decades will have profound implications for religious organizations and the total society, to say nothing of the elderly themselves as well as other new age groups from birth to death. The year 2020 will show a new constellation of the elderly and other age groups. Acting now on vital research and service needs in religion and aging with something approximating 20/20 foresight will be far better than waiting for the clarity of 20/20 hindsight.

To prioritize such future efforts in a research programmatic may be impossible and fruitless. Yet a few concluding remarks may be ventured.

1. Efforts should be intensified to build useful theoretical/theological models around which meaningful research could be organized. The model presented here may serve as an illustration.
2. There are three urgent areas for research presented in this model. The first has to do with the nature and role of spirituality in the lives of the elderly. The second concerns the role of organized religion in quality aging. The third involves the relations of these two and the other areas of research into the aging process and its implications for our changing culture, society, and physical worlds.
3. In order to facilitate these and other research priorities, some means need to be discovered or created to call the attention of scholars in gerontology and in religion to the importance of research in religion and aging and to support their research efforts. The positive rewards for researchers in gerontology and in religion would need to be enhanced considerably to get quality work accomplished in these areas. As already mentioned, these efforts could involve theological schools, an expansion of this journal, ecumenical agencies, centers for team research, and financial support from religious and secular sources. Ways would need to be explored to facilitate discussions and research work between specialists in different fields as well as between generalists and specialists.

Perhaps the most hopeful and optimistic evidence of future movements in these directions would be the positive interest and enthusiasm generated by this publishing venture.

What if we are on the Third Wave of Toffler[14] and swimming in the Megatrends of Naisbitt?[15] What implications do these future visions have on the prospects for quality aging? What about the needs for new research designs now to prepare for a rapidly growing population of older persons in a rapidly changing world?

Naisbitt believes that we are living in a time of parentheses between eras when we can have extraordinary influence "if we can only get a clear sense, a clear conception, a clear vision, of the road ahead" (p. 252). This unlikely scenario of research questions and possibilities is devoted to this vision of the future for the elderly and all who relate to them and who will become elderly in turn. Something of the optimism for the future is shared by Naisbitt in his closing words, "My God, what a fantastic time to be alive!" (p. 252).

NOTES

1. This tri-window approach may appropriately be used in research under three questions: What is the present situation (viewing); what was the past situation (reviewing); what may be the future situation (previewing). This may also frame the meditative practice of older persons individually or in groups.

2. Thomas C. Cook (ed.) *The Religious Sector Explores Its Mission to Aging* (Athens, Georgia: National Interfaith Coalition on Aging), 1976. James A. Thorson and Thomas C. Cook (eds.), *Spiritual Well-Being of the Elderly* (Springfield, Illinois: Charles C Thomas Press), 1980. *Theological Education*, "Education for Ministry in Aging: Gerontology in Seminary Training," Volume 16, Number 3, Special Issue, Winter, 1980.

3. William M. Clements (ed.) *Journal of Religion & Aging*, Volume 1, Numbers 1-4, 1984-1985.

4. Vincent John Fecher, *Religion & Aging: An Annotated Bibliography* (San Antonio: Trinity University Press), 1982.

5. James W. Ellor and F. Ellen Netting, Religion and Aging Bibliography (Xeroxed), 1986, 17 pp.

6. A much earlier version of this model appears in Earl D. C. Brewer, "Life Stages and Spiritual Well-being," pp. 99-111, David O. Moberg (ed.), *Spiritual Well-Being — Sociological Perspectives* (Washington: University Press of America), 1979.

7. Martin Buber, *I and Thou*, Second Edition, (New York: Charles Scribners Sons), 1958. George Herbert Mead, *Mind, Self and Society* (Chicago: University of Chicago Press) 1934. Alfred Schutz, *Phenomenology of the Social World* (Evanston: Northwestern University Press), 1967.

8. William James, *The Varieties of Religious Experience* (New York: Random House), 1902, p. 475f.

9. Societal interactions gave rise to religious phenomena for Durkheim. Emile Durkheim, *The Elementary Forms of the Religious Life* (New York: Collier Books), 1961, p. 462f.

10. James E. Birren and K. Warner Schaie, *Handbook of the Psychology of Aging*, Second Edition (New York: Van Nostrand Reinhold), 1955.

11. Robert H. Binstock and Ethel Shanas, *Handbook of Aging and the Social Sciences*, Second Edition (New York: Van Nostrand Reinhold), 1985.

12. Cabb E. Finch and Edward L. Schneider, *Handbook of the Biology of Aging*, Second Edition (New York: Van Nostrand Reinhold), 1985.

13. Appreciation is expressed to various scholars with whom I corresponded about the issues of this paper. This participation certainly indicated significant interest.

14. Alvin Toffler, *The Third Wave* (New York: William Morrow), 1980.

15. John Naisbitt, *Megatrends* (New York: Warner Books), 1982.

PART II: CRITICAL ISSUES

Introduction

In Part I, an holistic, global view of religion and aging in a changing world was addressed. In Part II, specific issues are examined in light of changing times. I asked the contributors to re-examine the topics with which they have become familiar, and speculate from this possible outcomes for the future. In short, I asked them to consider what the religious sector should know, and be prepared for, as we near the 21st century. What will be the response of religious communities and organizations as aging, and the problems and challenges accompanying it, confront them with its unavoidable realities?

Some may look at the table of contents for this section and draw the conclusion that a social problems approach has been taken with respect to aging and religion in the future. John Lindquist explores the strengths and challenges of a soon-to-be rich and poor (elderly) Baby Boomer generation. Tex Sample paints a picture of poverty for many future Americans now between twenty and sixty-five years of age. Barbara Payne suggests that sexuality and aging is no laughing matter. David Oliver takes a hard look at the abandonment of church/synagogue/parish members as they enter the world of the nursing home. Rabbi Ed Cohn alerts us to the realities of suicide as being most prevalent among those in the latter third of life. Harold Hinrichs calls for more inclusive and therefore more meaningful

103

worship experiences. O. Z. White calls religious communities to be more responsive to community needs.

The authors have raised issues which religious communities need to address if they are to make a significant contribution to the quality of life of future elderly Americans. The religious sector has always been concerned with social problems, and given the disproportionate number of older persons in the church/synagogue/parish, the response of this sector of society to the problems addressed here may determine not only the value accorded older persons, but it may also determine in part, whether or not the significance of religion itself will survive into the future.

Any religious professional (or group) reading this volume will find it difficult to continue with business as usual. Challenged by the realities which it poses for the church/synagogue/parish, the reader will be unable to avoid the implication that concerted action is not an option but a necessity.

The fact that religious professionals and religious bodies have not adequately addressed these issues in the past is no reason to assume that they are less worthy of attention in the future. Suicide has always been an age-related problem, and will be more so for the elderly in the 21st century. What does this say about the meaning and quality of living as the elderly experience it? Few things boost the morale and life satisfaction of an older person as does intimacy and sexuality. Yet, opportunities for intimate relationships in old age are limited. How then, particularly within the context of the church/synagogue/parish, can sex, aging and religion come together? Poverty is a symptom of a system of injustice. Why, in the midst of our free enterprise system, is poverty increasing? And why is it going to be so prevalent among the future elderly more so than it is today?

Age-segregation is just as ubiquitous in the church/synagogue/parish as it is in the larger society. The religious community is also race-segregated, sex-segregated and class-segregated. How do we break down the walls that divide us? How can religious communities become more inclusive? And what about older persons who have been allowed to disappear from the "religious family" as they are placed out of sight and out of mind in a nursing home? Will the Household be so extended so as to include these individuals? And finally, what about non-members? What is the responsibility of the religious sector to those in the community who cry out from oppression, poverty and depression? In short, will religious communities ask these hard questions and take a stand?

As stated earlier, if the religious sector cannot respond to these and other societal issues involving older persons, one wonders if the Baby Boomers will ever come back to the church/synagogue/parish. Indeed, the very relevance of religion, as we know it, may come under attack. And, if we continue to segregate older persons (as we do children) in the context of our worshipping communities, we may cut off the main vine which has, in the past, provided the foundation for our faith.

A community of faith cannot become isolated from the rest of the world. It cannot exist for itself, it must exist for others. All long-honored religious traditions proclaim this truth. It is, therefore, time to respond. I only hope it is not already too late.

David B. Oliver, PhD
Editor

Prognosis for the Future: Looking at the Past

John H. Lindquist, PhD

SUMMARY. The "Boomer" generation will begin to turn age 65 in 2011. This huge cohort represents both strength and a challenge to secular and religious institutions alike. A tip of the "Boomer" iceberg will be affluent. Many will be self-supporting. But a large number will be in need. A majority of the boomers are entering their prime earning years on a schedule that is actually behind that of their parents. Churches and denominations have 30 years to prepare to meet the needs of the Boomers as they enter old age.

THE CRISIS BEFORE US

Churches of all denominations in the United States are today the benefactors and at the same time the future moral custodians of those born in the 1946-1964 period; the Baby Boomers have come of age. The youngest is now 22 and the oldest 40; marrying, producing their own baby "mini-boom," fueling the economy as they enter the peak of their durable-goods purchasing years, having reached the threshold of their high-earning period. They are the market for cars, houses, washing machines, refrigerators, and all the high-tech, high-cost "adult toys" (video-cassette recorders, automated cameras, color television, stereo components).

More to the point of our concern, except for some denominations, they are joining churches, but not in the numbers anticipated. America's churches are in the midst of a membership stagflation, but still growing. When the baby boom was three years old (1949), 265,583 churches served 77,386,000 members. By 1959 the num-

---

John H. Lindquist is Professor of Sociology at Trinity University, San Antonio, Texas. His publications include a co-edited volume, *The Elderly: Victims and Deviants*. Among his current projects is a paper on the judicial disposition of elderly felons and misdemeanants.

107

ber of churches had increased by 14 percent (309,449) and membership by 30 percent, to 109,558,000. Today, 391,111 churches serve
139,603,000 members. Churches have been building nearly 30 million square feet of new construction annually for the past 15 years.
Religious organizations in the United States receive nearly half
(47.8% in 1983) of all charitable giving. This has increased precipi-
tously, as the Boomers have come of age. In 1955 churches received
$3.33 billion. Fifteen years later this had tripled to $9.30 billion. In
1983 this giving had more than tripled, to $31.03 billion. The num-
ber of Protestants, as a percentage of church preference expressed
by adults, has declined (69 percent to 56 percent of those who have
a preference) between 1947 and 1983, while the number of Catholics have increased (20 to 29 percent).[1]

The Boomers are also taking leadership roles as the generation of
the 1920's reaches retirement age. Between now and the end of the
20th century they will dominate churches just as they dominated
every aspect of American society; from maternity wards to schools
to the job market to the consumer market. Their sheer numbers,
some 78 million born between 1946 and 1964, have been a boon
and a burden to American society. Their spirit and numbers will
mold the churches just as they have every other institution of our
society. They represent a challenge to the churches just as they have
every other aspect of the social fabric. The Boomers have remade
America at every point along the life cycle. They are and will be
both a source of great strength and a major burden upon the social
structure as they contribute individually and collectively to individual churches and denominations during their working days and draw
upon these same churches and denominations in their golden years;
whether members or non-members, they will be people in need and
will be the stewards of the needy.

The thesis of this paper is that the challenge of the Boomers will
remake the churches of America, just as their presence has remade
the secular world. They are going to demand that churches accomplish two major tasks in a very short time-span: their secular needs
will require that churches more than ever before become involved in
the social and economic needs of the people and this will at the
same time require the churches to look outward as well as inward.

Churches have traditionally represented sanctuaries for their
members, providing for the spiritual needs of a narrowly defined
congregation. They have also sought, in a variety of ways, to use
their resources in charitable ways for those, whether churched or

not, who are economically depressed and, to focus upon the thrust of this paper, to service the needs of their members as they reach retirement age. These activities have targeted members of individual churches and denominations. One does not have to look far to discover a plethora of services, agencies and programs, designed to serve the elderly membership. The Hebrew Rehabilitation Center of Boston targeted physically and mentally deteriorated aged residents of a housing unit in a program designed to reawaken memories of prior religious practices.[2] Catholic Family Counseling, Inc., has created a special unit for older Catholics, "Special Services to Older Persons," in order to meet the needs of these older communicants.[3] Individual denominations build homes for their aged members, some as charity projects for those of low income, others designated for the financially independent. Individual denominations, such as the Lutheran Church in America, have sought to outline a ministry aimed at their aging members.[4] Literally tens of thousands of such efforts have been and are being made by churches and denominations as they seek ways to serve their elderly members. A very complete bibliography of nearly 500 annotated entries has been written as a guide to the literature related to religion and aging.[5] Many of the items detail the work of individual churches and denominations in the area of their elderly membership.

However noble these efforts, they will be overwhelmed by the magnitude of the problems produced by the Boomer generation. Their efforts to meet effectively the needs of this huge cohort will be seriously weakened by the "Baby Bust" that followed the "Baby Boom." Beginning in 1965, the annual number of births in the United States began to fall. These declining birth cohorts came to be called the "Baby Busters." If one imagines the two populations moving through the life cycle, one sees a very large cohort of Boomers preceding a smaller cohort of Busters, whose responsibility it will be to provide for the care of those Boomers who are unable to care for themselves. The Busters, as individuals, will be as unable to provide as will the churches to care for their members, individually. These two forces, the Boomers and the Busters, represent a challenge to the churches of America the like of which they have never faced before. The churches have 30 years to prepare themselves to face this monumental social issue. The response of the churches must, I believe, be three-fold: there must be, first of all, an increase in the efforts directed toward non-members, the traditional sanctuary approach will be inadequate to the task (30 percent of U.S. adults are non-churched); second, there must be a new ecumenical spirit so as to bring together the resources of the churches and denominations in order to maximize their combined contributions; and third, the churches must seek to influence secular institutions, particularly governments and social agencies at all levels, in order to force them to face the facts of social reality — a laissez faire approach to the social needs of the elderly will insure a disaster of extraordinary proportions. Warren Johnson wrote recently; "The goal of science is to *describe* reality; religion attempts to give it *meaning*, and to order life around this meaning." [6] In order to accomplish this, the churches must be able to assist secular leaders and secular institutions as they seek to relate to the facts of life associated with the needs of our future elderly population.

THE GRAYING OF AMERICA

There were nearly 25 million Americans (11.2 per cent of population) age 65 and over in 1980. The median age of the population was 30.2 years. When the new century begins there will be 34.9 million (13.0 percent of the total) and the median age will then be 35.5 years. By the third decade of the 21st century there will be 64.6 million (21.2 percent of the total); the median age will be 38. The number of persons age 65 and older will begin to decline after 2030, as will the median age; as the Boomers are replaced by the Busters. [7]

If we do not see a change in the birth rate and in immigration policy over the next decades (the only other factors besides death that can affect population size), the only age group which will increase significantly will be those over age 55.

There are important differences among the 65 and over age group; differences which have policy implications for Church and State. The Boomers, and Busters, can expect to live longer than previous generations; and live longer in better health. But, the huge size of the Boomer generation means that when even a portion of them are in poor health or in economic need, they represent a strain on the system that the system is not prepared to meet. The fastest growing age group in the United States is now those over 85. They now represent 38 percent of the over 65 group, but will be nearly half (47 percent) by 2035. We can expect, because of their better health throughout their lifetime, that seven of ten of the Boomers will reach age 65 (8 of 10 women). Those who reach 65 can expect to live another 14 years, if they are men and 18 if they are women.

The future for men and women will be different. Most men who reach age 65 live with their spouses. Women, on the other hand, are more often widowed and living alone. At the present time about 75 percent of the men and 37 percent of the women age 65 and over are married and living with their spouses. Only 16 percent of the men of this age and older live alone, compared to half the women. Widowhood is the future for women: today 20 percent are widowed by age 60, this becomes 60 percent by age 65 and 70 percent by age 75. By contrast, only 14 percent of the men are widowed by 65 and only 23 percent by 75. The most common topic of discussion among women in their 50's is how to plan for a future that includes the near-certainty of widowhood.

These are well-educated, active people, who have had and do now have, a political, economic and social impact on our society. There is no reason to believe they will become docile in old age. The Gray Panthers, with their motto, "Off Your Asses," are going to find their style of politics even more enlivened when the Boomers enter old age. Because the women, as well as the men, of this generation, are well-educated, many have entered the professions and businesses. Unlike their poorly-educated sisters of previous generations, they have participated in the emancipation of women and we can expect them to continue to play leadership roles in the future.

Throughout most of history the aged have been the controlling force in society. Industrialization destroyed that power. They lost control of the land when factories replaced agriculture. They lost control of education when schools replaced their wisdom. They became obsolete when new technologies made better goods at a faster pace. The coming of the Boomers increased the pace of change. Their numbers turned our heads in their direction. They were the market, the votes, the new communicants. They became our new guides. The elderly were ignored, or when portrayed in the media, presented as frightened, silly, sexless, creatures living fruitless lives and acting as a drag on society. What will happen when these youths who thrust aside the aged, to take center stage themselves, become aged? My guess is that these innovators who have confused us throughout their lives may continue to do so. They may remake the distinction between work and leisure just as today's technology is remaking the distinction between work and home. We are already seeing "non-traditional" students being courted by universities whose classrooms go unfilled by the small cohorts of the Busters. The Boomers may force us to rethink the concept of old age. Instead of being old at 65, they may, because of their better health, better education, and history of vigorous participation, simply redefine old age. Old may begin at 75 or perhaps 85, when physical decline is commonly accepted to become a serious problem. However they act, one thing is certain, the Boomers are going to have an impact as they enter the ranks of the elderly.

THE FAILED PROMISE

The Boomers began life at a time of extraordinary economic growth. They became the best fed, best educated, most pampered of all American generations. They were promised that the future was to be theirs. The Yuppies of the 1980's were to be the fruition of the promise. The Yuppies, however numerous and well publicized, are, unfortunately, only the tip of the iceberg. The Boomers, as did those who came before them, expected that they would live better than their parents. The reality is that they are not now and will not do so in the future, as a group. Their economic life, far from expanding in an exponential fashion, is, in actuality, deteriorating. There is an illusion of well-being, but it is dependent upon several factors continuing in place; both spouses must work, they must have fewer children to consume their income growth, they must purchase smaller homes than did their parents, and the ability of relatives to loan them money for the purchase of a home must continue to exist (in 1980 nearly one-third of all first-time home buyers received financial assistance from relatives. Less than 10 percent needed such assistance in 1978).[8]

When we compare the young adult of today, who will be the retired adult of the 21st Century, we find that, compared to their parents, they are, on the average, worse off. A 30 year old man, in 1959, saw his income rise 49 percent in ten years. A 30 year old man, in 1973 had his income drop by 25% by the close of 1984. The costs associated with providing the necessities of life have increased and are taking a larger share of personal income. In 1973, a 30 year old man paid 21% of his gross pay for a medium-priced house. This same man paid 44% of his gross income for that medium-priced house in 1984. Home fuel and utility costs have increased by 54% between 1973 and 1984. Young families in the 1980's save less than young families in the 1970's, have more debt, at interest rates 50% higher than a decade ago, and give less to charities than did similar families in the 1970's. America's middle-class, the backbone of our society and of our churches, is in trouble.[9] Their dollars do not buy what their parents' dollars bought. To see what this may very well mean for the future, let's look at the condition of today's elderly.

In 1983, 14.1% of persons aged 65 and over lived below the poverty level, 3,700,000 individuals. Another 8% were classified as near-poor (an income between the poverty level and 125% of this level). One of eight elderly whites was poor in 1983 compared to over one-third (36%) of elderly blacks and nearly one-in-four (23%) of elderly Hispanics. More elderly women (17%) than men (10%) live in poverty and more who live alone or with non-family members (26%) live in poverty compared to those who live in a family situation (8%).[10]

By 2010 there will be 34,800,000 persons in the U.S. age 65 and older. Their future economic condition depends upon their current condition, which is not as good as that of those who went before. It is not unreasonable to assume, then, that at least the same percentage of elderly will be living at a near poverty level in 2010 as now. Given the high unemployment rate of urban blacks and Hispanics, it is also not unreasonable to believe that more than one-in-three blacks will live in poverty in 2010. This leads me to conclude that there will be at least 4,906,800 persons age 65 and over living in poverty (14.1% of 34.8 million) at that date — a date which precedes the beginning of the traditional retirement age for the Boomers.

The Boomers, presently struggling to achieve and maintain middle-class status, represent a huge debt that must be paid. They are not going to be in as good a position to care for themselves as are their parents of today. They are dependent upon relatives for loans to buy homes. These relatives are dying. They will have more siblings, but they are their competition, not their potential benefactors. They are having fewer children than did their parents, and therefore fewer helping hands when they reach retirement. The federal government is retrenching rather than expanding assistance in the areas of housing, nutrition, medical care, and other social services at the very time when the Boomers are putting severe pressure on these services. This will put the local governments and non-governmental agencies under the gun, at a time when citizens are lobbying for tax freezes at the non-federal level and charitable giving is stable or on the decline.

These are the realities facing the leadership of today's churches and denominations. They must become advocates for the elderly, joining forces with the various organizations which lobby for their elderly members: American Association of Retired Persons, Gray Panthers, and groups representing various occupations and industries, e.g., teachers, federal employees, railroad engineers, veterans.

THE ISSUES

The unmet needs of the elderly are already a problem of monumental proportions. They are as nought compared to what will exist in the early decades of the 21st Century. Ignoring them will not make them go away. The churches and denominations of America must gird themselves today in order to begin the battle which will surely face them tomorrow. We are already in the midst of the crisis and we must work our way out of it or we will be overwhelmed. When the Boomers begin to reach retirement age, the solutions must be in place. We cannot wait until then to address the issues.

Housing

Currently 94% of non-institutionalized men age 65 and over live with their spouse (77%) or alone (18%). Six percent live with other relatives. Some 82% of non-institutionalized elderly women live with their spouses (39%) or alone (43%). Eighteen percent live with other relatives. Only 5% (1.2 million) elderly live in nursing homes. The proportion living in nursing homes increases dramatically with age. Seven percent of the 75-84 year olds live in nursing homes and 23% of those 85 and older.[11] The elderly of today are, to a great extent, living in homes they purchased during a period of low interest rates, relatively cheap housing costs, and low inflation. The Boomers have not been able to build equity in housing to the same extent as have their parents. Only 70% of the 30-35 age married couples own their own home. This percentage is expected to decline, according to the National Association of Realtors.[12] The Boomers are, more than the present generation of elderly, going to reach retirement age without a homestead. Their income is going to decline with retirement, and they will be in need of inexpensive rental housing. The number of elderly homeless is unknown today, just as the number of homeless of all ages. Federal estimates, hotly and widely disputed, are that there are 350,000 homeless Americans. Others, primarily those who operate shelters for the homeless in urban America, assert there are as many as 3 million homeless. We found that 3% of those seeking shelter in one emergency shelter operating in San Antonio in the winter of 1984-85 were over age 62. These street people are literally residing in boxes, under expressways, and wherever else they can find shelter. The federal government insists that there is no housing shortage in America, only a shortage of affordable housing for all. The Administration is seeking remedies which will be cost-effective, i.e., provide housing assistance at the lowest cost to the tax payer. This effort has failed to date and one can anticipate with a measure of certainty that shelter for the elderly will increasingly be a problem.

Medical Care

The elderly make disproportionate use of medical care facilities, compared to those under age 65. Approximately 18 percent of them were hospitalized in 1981, compared to nine percent of those under age 65. They stay in the hospital longer (10 days on average, compared to 7 days for younger Americans), and visit doctors more often (six visits per year compared to four). Various federal (Medicare), state (Medicaid), and other (insurance) programs, cover only 67% of their medical bills.[13] New, cost-saving features of Medicare and Medicaid will reduce the federal and state contribution. Most older persons have at least one chronic illness requiring maintenance medical care; many have more. It is estimated that a person who lives to age 85 will suffer from five chronic illnesses. The Boomers are going to live longer and ultimately, though they have benefited from better health throughout their lives, they will require great quantities of medical care. High-tech medicine is costly medicine. The end result is that the elderly poor will receive lower quality and less medical care than their better-off brethren unless we make drastic changes in our health care system. Recent changes in Medicare force hospitals to discharge patients early or accept financially ruinous losses. Most hospitals are for-profit, which means the public hospitals are going to have to expand greatly in order to meet the need, because for-profit hospitals refuse to admit patients without insurance. Elderly Americans today find the financial burden of medical care beyond them. Many forego buying basic health-related items—eye glasses, hearing aids, and prescription medicine. Many split dosages of maintenance prescription drugs in order to make the medication last longer. Medical doctors prefer not to specialize in geriatric medicine. Physicians can earn more from a fifteen minute surgical procedure than they can from providing care for the elderly. The needs of the elderly require time-consuming diagnostic examinations and continuing visits, which bring in less money than does serving younger patients with fewer complications. We do not now have enough geriatricians and will need ten times as many by the 21st century. We do not now have the money, the services, or the will to provide medical care for the elderly. We must find the money and see to it that services are available for the elderly of the future. We must find the will.

Care-Giving

Care-giving for the elderly has traditionally been the responsibility of the children of the elderly, usually daughters. But the demographics of the future mitigate against this continuing as the major source of care-giving. Unless the present potential parents drastically increase the number of children they will have, by 2030 there will be more people over 65 than between the ages of 18 and 64. The ratio of care-givers to the elderly is declining: in 1981 there were 51 persons age 80 and older per 100 persons the age of their children; by the year 2000 there will be 96 age 80 and older per 100 the age of their children. Many of the non-institutionalized need assistance in the performance of particular tasks, e.g., bathing, dressing, eating, using the toilet, getting in and out of chairs and bed, walking, going to and from church, shopping, meal preparation, money management, home repair. These elderly are able to remain in the community, which is preferable to institutionalization, as long as they can receive assistance in one or a few of these areas.

About 2.7 million elderly required assistance in 1980, about 11.5 percent of the non-institutionalized elderly (9 percent of males and 14 percent of the females). The percentage needing assistance increases with age; 7% of those 65-74, 16% of the 75-84 age group, and 39% of those age 85 and older. Presently about half of all functional assistance is being provided by children.[14] The demographics are such that this will not be the case in the future. The Boomers were born into large families and as long as younger siblings are able to provide care, they can rely upon them. But the Boomers as a generation are marrying less, marrying later, and having fewer children. They will require, more than any other generation, the assistance of non-family individuals and social agencies, if they are to remain non-institutionalized.

Nursing Homes

America's nursing homes are a national disgrace. The homes that provide excellent care are full and have waiting lists. Those that accept Medicaid patients who require more than ordinary care (the bedridden, for example) are overwhelmed, understaffed, and heavily criticized for the level of care provided. Between 1 January 1985 and 25 November 1985, in Texas, the state took 321 punitive actions against nursing homes (defined as cancellation of contract, decertification of facility, or withholding of payment) in that state. Horror story after horror story is to be found in the records of nursing home inspectors — malnutrition, dehydration, infected decubiti, missed meals, untrained and inadequate staff, overreliance on sedating medication, restraining the elderly in wheelchairs and beds, physical abuse, and more.

Federal and state agencies seem unable to supervise nursing homes and the homes operate from a position of strength; the 1985 vacancy rate was under five percent. There will be a continuing need for nursing homes in the United States; the lack of care-giving children, the lengthened life span of the Boomer generation, and the need for assistance, all lead one to conclude that nursing homes, in large numbers, will be required. Even if the nursing home population remains at five to six percent of the elderly, there is still a need for beds for four million Boomers, over three times the number currently residing in nursing homes.

CONCLUSIONS

If there is going to be any measure of dignity for millions of Americans who reach old age in the 21st century, the policies which foster it must be put in place soon. Churches, synagogues, denominations, etc., can play a significant role in formulating and implementing these policies and seeing to it that they are implemented. There must be innovation at every level of society. Pressure must be placed on public officials to get them to accept the fact that there is a massive social problem, not an individual problem, that must be addressed. Churches today labor mightily, give unstintingly, and perform charitably. Let them become even more innovative, not simply give more, because there is a limit to giving and the need is beyond their ability. Especially hard hit in the 21st century will be minority men and women. They, to a far lesser extent than their white brethren, are failing to achieve the American Dream of a home, a secure job, and protection for their old age. They work in low-wage, part-time, non-social security jobs. They suffer to a great extent from underemployment and unemployment; up to 50% of black youths are unemployed in our metropolitan areas; many grow to young adulthood having never held a full-time job. They participate less often in pension plans and are unprotected by medical insurance. It is not unusual today for churches to band together to provide ecumenical centers for emergency food, shelter, and clothing. It is also not unusual for one church to "adopt" another church of their faith, in order to provide assistance of one kind or another. These measures will need to be examined anew, perhaps crossing denominational and geographic boundaries to a greater extent than is done now. There are organizations that lobby for nursing home reform, and which serve as advocates for the elderly, in and out of nursing homes. One way to improve nursing home care is to provide continuous oversight; a relative visiting at a different time each day is better protection than the supposedly unannounced visit of a state inspector. Churches could "adopt" a nursing home in their area and provide continuous oversight. Individual residents could also be "adopted."

The first task is to recognize the problem. Once that is done people can act in such a way that they are able to contain the problem and eventually eliminate it. By the time we reach the 21st century we will be allocating half the federal budget to the care of the elderly. It will not be enough. Concerned individuals, alert and aware churches and denominations, and responsible state and local governments must accept a share of the responsibility, or the shame.

NOTES

1. See Statistical Abstract of the United States for statistics on church membership, buildings, and other information on churches in the United States.

2. Edith Abraams, "Religion in the Rehabilitation of the Aged," in James A. Thorson and Thomas C. Cook, Jr. (eds.), *Spiritual Well-Being of the Elderly* (Springfield, Illinois: Charles C Thomas, 1980), pp. 187-194.

3. Sister Maria Baptista, "A Missing Generation in Catholic Charities," *Catholic Charities Review*, 45 (February 1961): 5-10.

4. Martin Heinecker and Ralph Lellenich. *The Church's Ministry with Older Adults: A Theological Basis* (New York: Lutheran Church in America, Division for Mission in North America, 1976).

5. Vincent J. Fecher, *Religion and Aging: An Annotated Bibliography* (San Antonio: Trinity University Press, 1982).

6. Warren Johnson, *The Future is Not What It Used to Be* (New York: Dodd, Mead, 1985).

7. See Landon Y. Jones, *Great Expectations: America and the Baby Boom Generation* (New York: Coward, McCann and Geoghegan, 1980), for a concise history of the Boomers.

8. Maxwell Glen and Cody Shearer. "Dreams Have Gone Bust for Baby Boomers," *San Antonio Light*, 31 December 1985.

9. *Washington Post Weekly*, 23 December 1985.

10. See "A Profile of Older Americans: 1984," American Association of Retired Persons, Washington, D.C. N.D., p. 10.

11. *Ibid.*, p. 11.

12. Glen and Shearer, *op. cit.* 13. "A Profile of Older Americans: 1984," *op. cit.*, p. 14.

14. *Ibid*.

The Elderly Poor,
the Future,
and the Church

Tex Sample, PhD

SUMMARY. This paper examines the future of the elderly poor in the United States in the light of the impact of certain demographic, economic, and political trends presently in place. These trends are then projected for four generational groups now of "working age" in an attempt to discern the extent of poverty among the elderly of the future. If present trends continue, an ominous future awaits those Americans now between twenty and sixty-five years of age. The capacity of the Church to respond to this situation is discussed, and a variety of roles it can perform are suggested.

What is the future of the elderly poor in the United States? Are there demographic, economic, social and political trends which augur new hope or a deepening crisis for the nation's elderly poor? Are there strategies which could be effective in liberating the elderly from poverty? With the large number of older Americans in its ranks, what response can the church make to the plight of the elderly poor? These are the concerns to be considered here.

The discussion which follows is divided into four parts. The first is a review of recent trends in poverty and an assessment of the relative impact of the economy and social policy in determining these trends. Next is a delineation of major demographic, economic, social, and political factors which will determine, in great

Tex Sample is Professor of Church and Society at Saint Paul School of Theology, Kansas City, Missouri. He previously served as Pastor, Peoples United Methodist Church, Haverhill, Massachusetts, and Director of the Department of Social Relations, Massachusetts Council of Churches. He recently authored *Blue Collar Ministry: Facing Economic and Social Realities of Working People*, Judson Press, 1984.

part, how many people are poor and who they are. From these factors I will project future scenarios for four generational groupings in the U.S. who are now between twenty and sixty-five years of age. This third part of the paper, then, will attempt to depict the shape and size of poverty in the future should present trends continue. Finally, in the face of a challenge that is societal in scope, I will make suggestions for the role of the church in that broader range of effort required to break the hold of poverty on the elderly poor.

RECENT TRENDS IN POVERTY: THE ROLE OF THE ECONOMY AND PUBLIC POLICY

A fundamental debate has recently been joined about poverty, its pattern and causes and what can be done about it. Charles Murray's book, *Losing Ground: American Social Policy 1950-1980*, argues that the welfare programs established in the 1960s by the War on Poverty created dependency and induced many of the poor to remain so. He believes these assistance programs should be eliminated for those who are of working age and able to work. Meanwhile Michael Harrington maintains that more government assistance and new job programs are needed to respond to the new American poverty which resulted from structural changes in the nation's economy.[1]

This debate is of interest here not only because of what it says about the causes of poverty but also because of its implications for the future of poverty. If the basic causes of poverty relate to the structure of the national economy, then future projections need to give this dominant consideration. On the other hand, if a sizeable share of poverty is engendered by dependency — creating welfare policies, obviously, forecasts for the future will require a different set of trajectories. Therefore, the basis for the projections of this paper will turn on an assessment of which of these arguments is the more explanatory.

Recent trends overwhelmingly favor the explanation that change in the size and make-up of the poverty population are much more closely related to the economic well-being of the society than they are to social welfare policies. In fact, poverty trends in the U.S. for the past twenty-five years have followed economic trends. During the 1960s and early 1970s when the economy was strong, poverty sharply declined from 22.4% in 1959 to 11.1% in 1973, where it fluctuated at about this level until 1978. However, as the economy worsened in the late 1970s and early 1980s, the poverty level rose to 15.3% of the population in 1983.[2] Further support for this interpretation came with the upturn in the economy in 1984, when median family income was up 3.3%, the biggest rate of increase since 1972, and the poverty rate was down to 14.4% from the 15.3% of the year before.[3]

Support for the economic explanation can be found not only in the parallel trend lines of the economy and of poverty but also in terms of *who* is poor in the new American poverty. In a carefully-documented argument, William P. O'Hara demonstrates that between 1978 and 1983 poverty increased regardless of religion, age, sex, race or family status. His point is that if anti-poverty programs fueled the increased poverty, then this increase would be more evident among the groups prone to rely on welfare. Instead, he found the higher rates of increase in poverty among those *least* likely to be welfare recipients.[4]

Does this mean that welfare policy does not affect poverty levels? No, but it affects them in a different direction than Charles Murray suggests. There is no question, for example, that the government spending cuts of the Reagan administration have increased the numbers of poor people and have indeed made life harder for many people who were already poor when his administration came to office and who now live more deeply in poverty than before.[5] While estimates vary, it is likely that Reagan policies increased the numbers of the poor by about a million persons, not enough by any means to account for the increase of 10.8 million from 1978 to 1983. Moreover, the increases began before Reagan took office. What this clearly indicates is that while welfare policy can indeed have an effect, i.e., increasing the number of people who are poor by cutting assistance programs, the deeper and more pervasive problem is economic and not one of social welfare policy.[6]

One group where social welfare policy has had, perhaps, the greatest effect is on the elderly people where poverty trends have followed economic trends hardly at all in the past twenty-five years. The discussion which follows will indicate why.

Recent Trends in Poverty Among the Elderly

In recent years the elderly have not been as affected by changes in the economy as have other age groups. Because social security and related government programs have been pegged to the inflation rate, the elderly have received a massive share of Federal cash outlays and a sharp drop has occurred in the level of poverty among the elderly.

In 1959, 35.2% of those 65 years of age and older were poor. In 1983 14.1% of the elderly were poor. This 1983 figure is up from 13.9% in 1978, a small increase in comparison with the percentage of upturn in poverty rates generally. Still, there were 3.7 million poor elderly people in 1983, and another 2.2 million had incomes between 100 and 125% of the poverty threshold, the near poor.[7]

In spite of these gains, elderly women and blacks are disproportionately poor. The poverty rate for elderly white men in 1982 was 8.2%. For elderly white women, the rate was 17.5%, elderly black men 31.8%, and for black women 42.4%.[8] These differences reflect the pervasive racism and sexism of U.S. society. Specifically, they reflect a significantly lower participation in well-paying jobs, less benefits from a Social Security system based on earnings, and, in comparison with white males, a well-below-average participation in the pension programs of the society.

These trends in poverty suggest complex relationships between poverty, the economy, and social welfare policy. As has been demonstrated, the level of poverty in a society is far more dependent on the health of the economy than on any other factor, even though not all groups participate equally in these gains, e.g., women and ethnics. Moreover, social welfare policy did not contribute to dependency and deeper poverty, but was an extraordinarily successful means of reducing poverty among the elderly, even in the context of a declining and stagnant economy. Again, not all people participated equally in the advantages of such policies, especially those in lower paying jobs with small contributions to social security and also those without pensions.

I am interested in these relationships between poverty, the economy and social welfare policy not only for what they say about recent trends but also for the impact such relationships have over the life cycle of a generation and for the implications such relationships have for a generation's future. That is, if a generation lives out its life under the most favorable of these conditions, then its poverty will be significantly diminished in contrast to a generation that would live out its life cycle under considerably less-advantaged circumstances.

At the risk, then, of belaboring the obvious, let me suggest that the poverty level of a generation in its elderly years will depend on the following:

1. The proportion of a generation's "working life" spent in a healthy economy.
2. The percentage of good paying jobs a generation has, especially when social security benefits are based on earnings.
3. The percentage of people in a generation who have pensions.
4. The support ratio of "working age" people to the elderly people of a generation; i.e., strong social security assistance requires an adequate base of working age people to pay for such assistance.
5. The political strength of a generation based on the size of its electoral strength and thus its capacity to influence government policy.
6. Finally, the degree to which women and ethnics are able to share in the benefits of good jobs with adequate pay and pensions.

Given these rather obvious statements about the life cycle and their implications for a generation's level of poverty, it will be useful to examine a number of other trends in U.S. society which impend directly on the economy, social welfare policy, demography, and other factors. These will have major consequences for today's generations under sixty-five years of age, as shall be seen in section three below.

MAJOR FACTORS SHAPING THE FUTURE

The elderly years of today's young generations are being established today. In this section I want to look at major factors which already are at work shaping the life cycle of each generation. To be sure, the factors delineated here are not exhaustive, but they seem especially relevant to the destinies of tomorrow's elderly poor.

First is a demographic matter known as the "support ratio," that is, the ratio of the number of "working people" to the number of "retirement age" people. Because elderly people are primarily aided through publicly-funded programs, the number of working age tax and social security payers compared to those drawing benefits from these programs becomes very important. The trend is cause for concern. For example, in 1940 there were approximately eleven elderly persons for every 100 persons 18 to 64 years of age, and in 1960 there were almost 17. In 1980 there were still fewer than

19, and projections for 1990 and 2000 indicate about 21 elderly persons per 100 "working age" people. This suggests that the support ratio will not change radically from the present to the end of the century. In the year 2010, however, the baby boomers begin to reach 65, and there will be a one-to-three ratio with a little more than 33 elderly persons per every 100 of those working age. In 2050 there will be almost 38 elderly persons per 100, a ratio of almost two elderly persons for every five working age persons. Given the types of social security and assistance programs that the U.S. now employs, it simply will not be possible to sustain life styles above the poverty level for the great numbers of these persons.[9]

A second factor has to do with changes in the American economy and its occupational structure. The entrance of the baby boomers into the labor force posed a major challenge to the U.S., and between 1970 and 1980 the civilian labor force increased from a little less than 80 million to a little more than 104 million workers. It is a remarkable achievement to increase the size of a work force by 24 million jobs in ten years, but this still requires a more careful examination. While we hear much of the "New Information Society," the new technology and the dynamism of American enterprise, the fact is that the major increases in jobs are occurring in the service sector, where jobs pay the lowest wages and where the quality of the work experience is the least desirable. For example, 13.2 million jobs have been created since 1973. Of these, private services accounted for 12.3 million, public services created 2.2 million, and industry *eliminated* 1.3 million. The major hirings were as secretaries, cashiers, vocational nurses, and cooks. Meanwhile, 170,000 jobs came from advanced technology and 120,000 of these were in data processing. "According to a prediction by the U.S. Bureau of Labor Statistics, in about ten years the service industries will be employing 73 percent of the work force (as against 53% in 1950 and 70% in 1984) with the highest growth . . . " in jobs like security and cleaning, sales and cashiering, fast food jobs and table waiting, secretaries, vocational nurses and nurses.[10]

Behind this boom in service jobs is the rapid growth of a large number of precarious, temporary, and often part-time jobs that offer no union protection, at the expense of stable, full-time jobs with labor management agreements. In 1984, the average weekly earnings for service workers was $248, about $12,000 per year.[11]

The point is this: the growing structural changes in the economy and in service occupations mean that an increasingly larger proportion of Americans will be employed in jobs that have little or no pensions, of which many are not covered by Social Security. Those workers which are covered will be paying less into the program and thereby receiving less when they retire. With the large numbers of persons employed in service sector jobs and with the anticipated increase of large numbers of elderly persons after the year 2010, when these generations become elderly, we will see a structural increase in the number of elderly people who are poor and near-poor.

Doubtlessly, one answer to this problem is extension of gainful employment beyond the age of 65, but this raises a third factor of considerable importance: the quality of work. If people must extend their working lives, then the quality of the work needs to be improved. Actually, this improvement will require a reversal of present trends. Bluestone and Harrison contend that the quality of "employment" has dropped significantly in the past 15 years. Two-thirds of the jobs created since 1970, in contrast to 45% which existed 15 years ago, require no professional qualification and pay less than $13,600 per year.[12] Such changes lead to a dual structuring of work: one arena which is decreasing in size, wherein work is vocation, a source of professional and social identity; and the other which is increasing in size, wherein work is necessity, a means of survival that does not provide meaning, honor, or vocational respect.

A fourth factor is the declining productivity of the U.S. economy. In the century before the mid-1960s industrial output per person employed in this country's manufacturing industry tended to increase at about three percent per year. However, from 1965 to 1970 that output dropped to 2.1%. Between 1970 and 1975 it dropped to 1.8%, and it fell to 1.7% between 1975 and 1980. These were the lowest annual rates of productivity ever for U.S. manufacturing and the lowest rates of productivity growth in any major industrialized country for which data are available.[13] Unless such productivity losses are turned around, it is difficult to see how the U.S. can provide adequately for the elderly in the twenty-first century, and what is inadequate for most gnaws at the very heart of subsistence for the poor and the near-poor.

A final factor, and good news at that, is the growing numbers of the elderly who represent *votes*. Older people tend to be more active as voters than are young persons. This provides an important source of power. In the 1980 election 71% of those between 55 and 64 years of age voted, and 69% of those in the 65 to 74 age group voted. This figure, however, fell to 58% for those who were 75 and older. In contrast, 40% of those under 25 voted, 55% of those 25-34, 64% of those 35 to 44, and 68% of those 45 to 54. [14] As the numbers of elderly grow in the 21st century, their electoral strength will be an important check and balance over the power of their younger contemporaries. This does not necessarily represent support for the poor, however, because government benefits in the recent past — when there has been a strong elderly vote — have gone mostly to the middle class. "The value of benefits going to the poor has fallen . . . and these benefits were not large to begin with." [15]

THE GENERATIONAL GROUPINGS AND THE FUTURE

In order to look now at the future I will break down the American population into a number of distinct generational groupings. [16] Each of these groupings will first be described as a unit, and I will then project implications for the elderly poor in each. The future of the elderly and the elderly poor will be greatly influenced by the opportunities of these generational units.

The World War II Generation

The first group is the World War II Generation. This is not an altogether satisfactory label, but these are the people who were roughly 50 to 65 years of age in 1985 and for whom World War II is a vivid image. Not only were they conscious of it, but they typically benefitted from the affluence which followed it. Most of them knew the Depression, at least something of it, and they saw the leap in affluence in the 20-year period following the war when the median family income more than doubled in constant dollars. [17]

Because immigration had slowed and because women had fewer children beginning in 1925, the World War II Generation was numerically small. Most of this generation — not all — matured in a world of increasing opportunities. Inexpensive housing awaited them — so much so that three-fourths of them owned their own homes, and half their homes were mortgage-free. Meanwhile their housing has significantly increased in value. Thirty-three million strong, a full 80% of this generation is covered by Social Security and 60% have pensions.

What does the future bode for this group? Some suggest that they may be the first affluent elderly when they reach the 1990s. To the degree that their sources of retirement income are indexed to the Consumer Price Index, this generation will not be radically affected by changes in the economy, certainly not to the degree of those under 65. Moreover, this group had the lowest rate of poverty of any group of age cohorts in 1984, under 10%. [18]

Nevertheless, this *is* a group in which 20% do not have social security and 39% do not have pensions. This generation — unless new policies are introduced — will experience what the elderly presently do in the United States where there are really two elderly populations. One is the group that is fairly comfortable, if not affluent, made up primarily of white males and mostly white couples. These are the skilled employees of the large corporations who not only draw pensions but receive the largest Social Security payments by virtue of benefits based on earnings.

The second group is populated mostly of minorities and single women, most of whom are widows. In this group, presently, almost half have incomes below the poverty level and the remaining majority have incomes that place them in the near-poor or marginal category (125% of the poverty index). These poor and near-poor elderly live at a subsistence level with no margin for emergencies. This group requires the most support in social service. When social services are cut, as they have been in recent years, this is the group that feels those cuts most severely. [19]

In this same connection, it needs to be remembered that the overwhelming outlays of government assistance go to the middle class. More than that, in recent years the benefits going to the poor have decreased in spite of the fact that they were not large to begin with. [20] "As social insurance cash assistance has been rising, cash assistance to the poor has been falling." [21] The point is that most of the World War II Generation should live their lives in reasonable comfort, barring economic collapse, nuclear devastation or some unforeseen event of similar magnitude. The poor and the near-poor of that generation have no such assurance, and present trend lines are moving against them.

The Between Generation

Born in the late 30s and early 40s this generation is 40 to 49 years of age. By "between" I mean that relatively small group of age cohorts born between the World War II Generation and the Baby

Boomers. Their "timing" has not quite given them the advantage of the older generation, and they are pushed from behind by the better-educated baby boomers. These Americans begin to reach 65 years of age in 2001. They will be pressed to retire early by the baby boomers; however, troubles in social security and other government programs could extend their working lives to 70 or beyond.

This generation began the year Social Security was enacted into law. They begin to reach 65 in 2001. In 2010, when they are 65 to 74 years of age, they will number over 20 million, constitute 7.2% of the total population and will represent a little over half of the elderly.[22] This generation will probably not begin to retire until 2005, or even later, because of the necessity of extending retirement. And this will delay the impoverishment of many of them. The fact that they will have spent their entire lives in the Social Security System should help, although it is impossible for the Social Security system to be operative as it presently is with the challenges the 21st century poses to it. Perhaps by then, as well, ethnics and women will have made greater strides in reducing inequalities in the employment, social security, and welfare systems, although no such changes are automatic but rather will require sustained political struggle. The well-being of this group, however, depends very much on developments in the international and domestic economic arenas. A strong economy could sharply reduce poverty; a weak one could be devastating for the elderly poor, especially in the face of the burgeoning numbers of people 65 and over in the society and the reduction of the support ratio of "working age" to "retirement age" persons. That there will be elderly poor and near-poor, nevertheless, seems inevitable if the United States continues in the direction of a service-oriented society. Should the deindustrialization of the U.S. have gone on apace, we could well see what some writers visualize as the "South Africanization" of the U.S., "permitting a well-off minority to purchase growing quantities of personal domestic services from an ever growing and poorly paid work force that subcontracting businesses provide to well-off households."[23]

Because this generation benefitted from the economic affluence of the late fifties, sixties, and early seventies, they will be more advantageously placed, as a generation, than the baby boomers who follow them. The better-educated baby boomers, however, will place increasingly competitive pressure on the Between Generation in the workplace.

The First Wave Baby Boomers

Almost eighty million strong, nearly one American in three is a baby boomer, that generation born between 1945 and 1965. There is a significant difference, however, between the baby boomers who are in their 30s and those in their twenties. Hence, I shall call the former the First Wave Baby Boomers and the latter the Second Wave Baby Boomers.[24] The median income of First Wave *couples* is $31,000, and 70% of these women are in the work force outside the home with an expected 80% employed by 1990. Two-thirds of the couples own their own homes and in 1983 had an average equity of $46,000. Their monthly mortgage averages $450 compared to an average of $794 for buyers in 1985.[25]

These figures for couples, however, can be deceptive because they do not reveal sharp differences between men and women and between whites and blacks. For example, the median income in 1984 for males betwen the ages of 30 and 34 and between 35 and 39 was $20,269 and $24,003 respectively. The comparable figures for women were $9,987 and $8,762.[26] Black men, as a whole, have a median income of $9,448, and black women have one of $6,164. Single baby boomers, especially women, will have a difficult time earning the median family income of $26,433. Blacks, single or couple of any age, will find it equally or even more frustrating.[27]

The First Wave Baby Boomers begin to reach 65 in 2010, and by 2020 they will be 65 to 74 years of age. They will constitute almost 30 million Americans and represent 10% of the total population. White males and couples who have pensions and some kind of government social security program should be comfortable. Those who do not, failing new and adequate social policies, face impoverishment. Moreover, these First Wave Baby Boomers will see a support ratio of one person "retirement age" for every three persons "working age" in 2025.[28]

In spite of their relatively more privileged position than the Second Wave Baby Boomers, the First Wave will have a significant number who have spent their lives in the service sector of the economy. These, along with others who have spent their lives in poverty and near-poverty, will struggle for subsistence. Given the present state of our economy, the enormous indebtedness of the U.S. government worsened by recent military spending, and our current social security and welfare policies, the 21st century looks forboding, indeed. It looks even worse for the Second Wave of Baby Boomers.

The Second Wave Baby Boomers

This group of Americans in their twenties entered the job market just as the economy was turning sour. The First Wave got the jobs and the housing and, by demand, helped to drive up housing costs. The oil crisis, inflation, unemployment, declining productivity, the departure of U.S. industry overseas, the rise of the service sector in the job structure, loss of confidence in the future, etc. led to a stagnant American economy. Real wages stopped growing in the U.S. in 1973 only to reverse slightly in 1983 and 1984. At present, this is a downwardly mobile generation.

The table below reveals the differences in median income by age and sex. Americans in their twenties have the lowest incomes of all except those 65 and over and women 60-64. Note also, however, that the median incomes of women remain basically unchanged from the time a woman is 25 years old until she is fifty, and then the income declines. Such statistics bode ill for the future in light of today's growing feminization of poverty.

Age, Sex and Median Income

Age

20-24	25-29	30-34	35-39	40-44	45-49	50-54	54-59	60-64	65 +

Male Med. Inc.

| $ 8,046 | $16,336 | $20,269 | $24,003 | $25,236 | $25,094 | $23,996 | $21,680 | $17,372 | $10,450 |

Female Med. Inc.

| $ 5,911 | $ 9,355 | $ 9,439 | $ 9,569 | $ 9,553 | $ 9,443 | $ 8,341 | $ 7,277 | $ 6,500 | $ 6,020 |

Source: Bureau of the Census. 29

In 1985 over half of the Baby Boomers made less than $10,000 per year, one-third of the men and two-thirds of the women. The great majority of these are the baby boomers in their twenties. It is this Second Wave that has entered the job market during the sharpest escalation of the service sector. This occupational life-line with its oppressive pay scales and penurious to non-existent benefits will dog these baby boomers throughout their lifetimes.

The Second Wavers reach 65 years of age in 2020 and will be 65 to 74 years of age in 2030. They will then number more than 34 million and will be 11.3% of the total population, moving the support ratio above the three-to-one level.[30]

Unless the U.S. in the next 30 to 40 years experiences great prosperity broadly distributed, and unless new directions in social welfare policy for the poor and near-poor are developed, the country
will experience the deepest poverty in a hundred years. In all likelihood, such poverty will be experienced by a burgeoning elderly
population that spent its working life on barely sufficient earnings,
if that, and will spend its retirement years on less than subsistent
government expenditures and grossly inadequate and condescend-
ing charity.

THE RESPONSE OF THE CHURCH

How can these scenarios be changed? Indeed, is there any hope,
and what role can the church play in the coming years to cancel out
the impoverished future which awaits many of tomorrow's elderly?
Except for immigration into the United States, especially by Hispanics and Asians, the demographic picture is basically in place.
Any strategy will have to work, for the most part, within the parameters of the age distribution of our population as it is. Therefore, the
two central arenas for strategic intervention seem to be in economics and politics. That is, new directions must be found to redi-
rect the trends of the economy, its occupational structure, its productivity, and its distribution of income. Such directions mean not
only economic change, but political will, which requires large social movements and citizen organizations. Such political will can
affect not only social policy but economic realities as well.
    The church's access to economic leverage points is largely re-
mote, but its contact with the grassroots in communities across the
U.S. is an important ingredient in its role in social change, as we
shall see.

The Strategic Location of the Church

In the U.S. there are more than 500,000 local churches and synagogues with more than 140 million members. "These institutions
provide substantial services to older persons in such diverse areas
. . . as transportation, counseling, education, fellowship, nutrition,
health care, housing assistance, home visiting, and volunteer service opportunities."[31] Moreover, elderly persons are the most religious people in the society when that is measured in terms of church

affiliation and in terms of their responses to questions about (a) the influence of religion on their personal lives; (b) a commitment by them to put religious beliefs into practice; and (c) the personal comfort and support they draw from religion. [32]

In addition, there has been a significant "graying" of the church in recent years with older Americans overrepresented. [33] In strategic terms social change typically requires a social vehicle, a group of people who are organized, who share or can share common values and interests, and who have the communication and organizing capacity to make an impact on the wider society. No institution is in a more advantageous place here than is the church. When the church joins with the many organizations of older Americans in common cause, they together can launch a significant measure of influence in the society.

Where Strategy Begins

Crucial to a strategic response by the church is the question of where such an effort begins. It cannot begin in some abstract and deducted set of programs developed out of the air by social planners and demographers, as important as their work is for disclosing the parameters of the challenge before us. Rather, an effective strategy is one that issues from the situation of the elderly poor themselves. In the flesh and blood, lived reality of their experience can be found fruitful directions for social change. A church strategy that emerges from the elderly poor and out of the praxis of confronting the deprivations and constraints of their lives is a requirement for concrete and effective social change. This requires an organized and active involvement of the elderly in shaping the future where they become resources for the discovery of what needs to be done and how.

Part of the problem here for the elderly poor is that the people served by the church are in large part middle class and affluent people. There can hardly be much question about the middle class bias of most of the churches. Even so, significant numbers of poor and near-poor people can be found in virtually every denomination. The National Opinion Research Center did a five-year study, 1974-1978, and found a sizeable percentage of lower-class people in major denominations. [34] Because elderly people are overrepresented in the church, such findings indicate a sizeable number of elderly persons who are poor and near-poor in major U.S. denominations. The point is that the church has already within its membership large numbers of the elderly poor and near-poor. It has access. What is needed then is an identification with the elderly poor by the church and a commitment of resources in their behalf.

The Roles of the Church

In order to be an effective part of the social effort required to address the economic and political challenges confronting an aging society, the church will find itself actively involved in at least four key roles. In many churches these roles will require a reordering of their mission and ministry.

The first of these roles can be called *the interpretive* function of the church. Having better access to the grassroots elderly and elderly poor than any institution in the society, the church has a heavy responsibility to interpret "the signs of the times," to increase awareness of the demographic, economic, and policy trends and their impact on the lives of their congregations. This is a conscious ness-raising task of major proportions, and it involves not only the elderly but the younger members as well whose destinies are already being set in place. Scenarios such as those advanced above can have a unitive impact on a congregation and provide opportunity for young and old alike to work on issues vital to their lives and to those of other generations.

Basic to this interpretive role is the task of futuring. Most churches do very little planning for the future much beyond five years, if that. The kinds of issues raised here, however, strike at the very lives of many church people and active attention to them can mean the difference between poverty and economic well-being for literally millions of people. Increasingly, then, local churches will have opportunity to provide seminars, special lesson series in church school, sermons, and other events as exercises in futuring. Massive consciousness raising is necessary for the emergence of social movements powerful enough to shift the economic focus described here. To be sure, some of this interpretation and futuring has already occurred, and many people are impressed by the demographic realities; but sufficient recognition of the economic trends and their implications for the elderly and the poor has not yet happened.

Within this interpretive role the church, along with others, has an important ideological task. By ideology I mean simply a world view with policy implications. Presently many Americans, impressed by currently popular images, view the U.S. as moving toward "the information society." The implications of such a world view suggest that the loss of industrial capacity and the jobs attendant thereto are merely concomitants of the megatrends of a new future. Such views need the rigorous application of "a hermenutics of suspicion" in order to see the long range implications of the information society for people in the United States and the devastating poverty destined for many. Doubtlessly, technology and communications will play an important role in the future; but if this occurs in a society where most people work in low-paying service jobs with relatively small contributions to Social Security and most without pensions, the range and the depth of poverty for the increasing numbers of elderly persons will take on unprecedented proportions.

Secondly, the church has an *advocacy role* to perform, meaning by that the function of influencing social policy through legislative action and lobbying efforts. In the civil rights movement the church proved to be an effective force in changing national law and policy. In that action there was a large constituency of citizens in the black community and a deep religious and moral legitimation for the goals of the movement. These factors, along with courageous leadership at significant ecumenical and denominational posts and the mobilization of many laity and clergy, made it possible for the church to make a key contribution.

The elderly presently compose a constituency about the size the black community was then and will increase in sizeable numbers in the coming years. Moreover, there is more support and considerably less resistance nationally to assisting the elderly than there was to the civil rights movements, as is evidenced by major Federal expenditures over the past twenty-five years. Add to this the electoral power of the elderly and the long-term interests of any citizen who expects to live beyond sixty-five, and the result is a formidable political force. Such a constituency requires carefully constructed coalitions, a savvy "feel" for the American political atmosphere, and a realistic sense for what the future portends. If the church will stick closely to the elderly and especially the elderly poor, if its strategic sense comes from a clear identification with the poor, it can play an important advocacy role.

Closely related to advocacy is a third role of *organizing*. Strong organizations of the elderly can demand services tailored and adequate to their needs. Such organizing is especially needed among ethnics and women who are most likely to struggle with poverty in old age.

In addition, there is an important organizing role to be done with working age persons in the service and low-income sectors of the occupational structure. Most of these people are not unionized, and labor organizations are currently experiencing tough times. Yet it is clear that regardless of what happens, many Americans will be employed in service and low-income jobs, and higher wages, benefits and pension programs will not come to such workers without strong labor organizations. Given the sheer size of this occupational sector, it could be the primary locus of labor organizing in the future. Again, the church needs to identify with persons in this sector, to focus evangelism especially on such persons, and provide religious and moral support for their organizing efforts.

Fourthly, the church can experiment with the role of *building alternative institutions*. Specifically, experimentation with non-profit, socially-owned residences and nursing homes. These could seek government and private funding and, as a matter of policy, provide space for a certain ratio of people who are poor. In some communities churches have cooperated with other groups in establishing community-owned businesses and factories. There has been enough success with these to encourage further experimentation and effort. These could model new management and income distribution procedures. Finally, given the rising costs of medical care, experimentation with community-owned health systems deserves careful study and consideration. This is obviously not an exhaustive list but suggests the possibilities for alternative institutions and organizations as an experimental function of the church and other community groups.

CONCLUSION

Certain demographic, economic, and social policy trends traject an ominous future in the 21st century with strong possibilities for large numbers of poor people in the elderly population. The difficulty of these problems mounts with the passing of time, and adequate solutions need to begin now. These solutions are primarily economic and political in character. While the church is more remote from the economic changes required, it has far more opportunities for action politically. By being closely identified with the elderly and the elderly poor and by developing strategies out of a context of human struggle, the church can be one effective agent in that range of people-based organizations and institutions who seem to be the best hope against the horizon of the 21st century to eradicate the poverty that awaits literally millions of today's generations.

NOTES

1. Charles Murray, *Losing Ground: American Social Policy 1950-1980* (New York: Basic Books, 1984); Michael Harrington, *The New American Poverty* (New York: Holt, Rinehart and Winston, 1984).

2. William P. O'Hara, "Poverty in America: Trends and New Patterns," *Population Bulletin*, 40, 3 (June, 1985), 3.

3. Bureau of the Census, "Money Income and Poverty Status of Families and Persons in the United States: 1985," *Current Population Reports*, Series P-60, No. 149, August 1985, p. 1.

4. O'Hara, "Poverty in America . . . ," p. 20.

5. *Ibid.*, 9.

6. Another significant factor here is that most government assistance goes to the middle class and not to the poor. See *Ibid.*, 25-26.

7. *Ibid.*, 5.

8. U.S. Senate Special Committee on Aging in Conjunction with The American Association of Retired Persons, *Aging America: Trends and Projections* (184), p. 36.

9. *Ibid.*, 8.

10. André Gorz, "The American Model and the Future of the French Left," *Socialist Review*, Trans. Carl Hathwell, 15, 6 (November-December, 1985), 102.

11. Bureau of the Census, *Statistical Abstract of the United States, 1985* (Washington, D.C.: U.S. Government Printing Office, 1984), p. 417.

12. Barry Bluestone and Bennett Harrison in the *International Herald Tribune* (June 20, 1984). Quoted in Gorz, "The American Model . . . ," p. 103.

13. Melman, Seymour. Testimony before the Task Force on Economic Policy and Growth of the Committee on the Budget, U.S. Congress (December 7 and 9, 1984), p. 88.

14. U.S. Senate et al., *Aging America*, p. 93.

15. O'Hara, "Poverty in America . . . ," p. 25.

16. Cheryl Russell, "Will You Be Rich?" *The Kansas City Star Magazine* (June 23, 1985), pp. 8-11 and 13. I am indebted to Russell's breakdown of contemporary "working age" generations.

17. Daniel Yankelovich, *New Rules* (New York: Random House), p. 21.

18. Bureau of the Census, "Money Income . . . ," p. 26.

19. Thomas B. Robb, Testimony before the Subcommittee on Oversight and Subcommittee on Public Assistance and Unemployment Compensation of the Committee on Ways and Means, U.S. House of Representatives, September 20, 1984, p. 91.

20. O'Hara, "Poverty in America . . . ," p. 25.

21. *Ibid.*, 30.

22. U.S. Senate et al., *Aging America*, p. 5.

23. Gorz, "The American Model . . . ," p. 105.

24. These labels are those of Russell, "Will You Be Rich?"

25. *Ibid.*, 8.

26. Bureau of the Census, "Money Income . . . ," p. 16.

27. *Ibid.*, 15-16.

28. U.S. Senate et al., *Aging America*, p. 8.

29. Bureau of the Census, "Money Income . . . ," p. 16.

30. U.S. Senate et al., *Aging America*, p. 8.

31. U.S. Senate et al., *Aging America*, p. 97.

32. *Ibid.*, 97.

33. Dean R. Hoge and David A. Roozen (eds.). *Understanding Church Growth and Decline, 1950-1978* (New York: The Pilgrim Press, 1979), p. 45f.

34. Quoted in H. Paul Chalfant et al., *Religion in Contemporary Society* (Palo Alto, California: Mayfield Publishing Co., 1981), p. 386. Chalfant et al. found the following percentages of lower class people in these denominational groupings: Baptists (31.7%), sects (25.6%), Catholics (23.5%), Methodist (23.3%), Presbyterians (20.0%), Jewish (15.2%), Lutheran (11.2%), and Episcopalians (5.4%).

Sex and the Elderly:
No Laughing Matter in Religion

Barbara P. Payne, PhD

SUMMARY. Two persistent myths about aging are that sex is for the young and religion is for the old. Contrary to these popular beliefs, adults do not necessarily turn to religion as they age nor do they lose sexual interest or cease to be sexually active. This paper examines sex, gender and sexuality of the elderly in relation to religious beliefs and church/synagogue participation. Five megatrends related to sex and aging and their implications for the church/synagogue are discussed: (1) from youth to adult congregations — the demographic imperatives; (2) from male to female congregations; (3) from married to single; (4) from either/or to multiple choice; and (5) from exclusive to inclusive.

When Abraham, a man of 100 years, and Sarah, a woman of 90 years, were told they would have a son, they both laughed — not because of Abraham's age, but because of Sarah's age.[1] In the Old Testament, it is not considered unusual for a man to father a child after he is 100 years of age. It was the limits of the child-bearing age for the female that made the possibility of mothering a child at the age of 90 a laughing matter.[2] Perhaps this ancient biblical account is the first recorded incidence of sex differences in aging and the sexual activity of older persons being viewed as a laughing matter.

Given the biblical bases for longevity and continued sexual activity, it seems strange that in 1986 sociologists' research confirming that older people fall in love in the same way that young people do would appear in *Psychology Today* and a syndicated Associated Press article,[3] and that birthday cards, cartoons and jokes would continue to make the sex life of older adults a laughing matter.

Barbara P. Payne is Professor of Sociology and Director of the Gerontology Center at Georgia State University, Atlanta, GA 30303-3083.

Even more difficult to understand is the omission of references to the sexual interests and needs for intimacy of older adults in denominational literature. Although the denominations have responded with programmatic books, they have given little or no attention to sexuality or sex differences in the age structure of their membership. An exception is Beecher's guide for clergy and congregations in ministry with older persons. He includes a short but excellent section on "the masculine-feminine polarity."[4]

While the Bible, science fiction writers and gerontologists treat the sexuality of older persons more positively than do religious writers and denominational leaders, gerontologists have given little attention to the role of religion and participation among the elderly.[5] As a consequence, the two most persistent myths about aging are that sex is for the young and religion is for the old. Contrary to these popular beliefs, adults do not necessarily turn to religion as they age,[6] nor do they lose sexual interest or cease to be sexually active. However, religious sanctions and beliefs about sexual behavior and negative social attitudes about the sexual needs of older persons do affect the way older people respond to their sexuality.

The sexuality and religiosity of older persons are usually addressed separately. We propose to examine sex differences in aging, sex roles and behavior of older adults in relation to religious beliefs and participation. We have identified for this purpose five megatrends to serve as a framework for the analysis of sex and aging and their implications for the church/synagogue in the future.

In everyday usage, sex and religion are used to describe a range of characteristics and behaviors. Sex is used interchangeably to refer to all sexual characteristics, identity, gender roles and behavior. For most social scientists, sex refers to the two mutually exclusive biological and physiological characteristics of the male and female; gender designates the behavior associated with enacting roles ascribed by society to males and females along with an individual's own sexual identity, i.e., feminine or masculine; and, sexuality refers to the emotional and physical responses to sexual stimuli.

Religion is the popular term that refers to personal religiosity, religious practice, and organizational participation. The social scientist studying religion and aging usually differentiates between religiousness, personal faith or non-institutional religious responses and religious participation in formal religious organizations. The social scientist's usage of sex and religion will enable a more discrete identification of the trends which will impact the church/synagogue.

FROM YOUTH TO ADULT CONGREGATIONS:
THE DEMOGRAPHIC IMPERATIVE

In less than 20 years we have moved from a youth society to an aging society. In 1986, the acceleration of this age shift gained public attention. As Baby Boomers (born between 1945-1960) began to turn 40, headlines in the business section of the Atlanta Constitution announced that "The World Is Not Just For The Young; Atlanta's Median Age is 31.1."[7] For the first time in U.S. history there were as many people over as under 30 years of age. The trend that the Baby Boomers will set is projected to raise the median age nationally to 36 by the year 2000 and to age 42 by the year 2050.[8] Equally as dramatic is the report that the fastest growing segment in the population is over 85 years of age and that this demographic trend is expected to continue.[9] Traditionally, churches/synagogues have been youth and couple oriented. Even though churches have been graying at a greater rate than the U.S. population, the shift to an adult or an intergenerational orientation is occurring at a slower pace within congregations than in the public and business sectors.

The membership for Protestant denominations is estimated to range from 37-47 percent over the age of 55. Furthermore, most major denominations can expect an unprecedented high rate of clergy retirement in the next ten years.[10] Consequently, as the congregations age the active clergy will be younger. This trend will make it essential for seminary education to include gerontological content and an emphasis on intergenerational relationships.

Most of the Judeo-Christian national organizations are awakening to the age shift in their membership. However, the responses seem to be focused mostly on social service needs and age specific programs. The time has come to address the continued need for intimacy and affirmation of sexual identity and activity throughout adult life — into the biblical over 100 years of age. Adult members, especially the Baby Boomers, who have experienced the sexual revolution will provide the impetus for more education within the context of their religious faith on human sexuality in the mid-to-late life.

Although the Baby Boomers have been the more sexually liberated as young adults, they are unlikely to be prepared for or to understand the age changes in sexual performance and opportunities. Many will believe that sex after sixty is a laughing matter — when it refers to their parents. When they are over sixty it will be a serious matter. As the Baby Boomers experience the age changes, they will seek reliable information about life stage intimacy needs and performance. They will be the leaders of an aging sexual revolution in which continued sexual activity will be a normal expectation, not the subject for jokes.

Gerontologists have known for some time that most older people are sexually active. While age has been identified as the most important factor affecting frequency and the form of sexual activity, there is no physiological basis for predicting inevitable sexual dysfunction accompanying aging. On the contrary, the Duke Longitudinal Research study found that, for some older persons, sexual interest and activity actually increase with age.[11] These gerontological research findings need to be utilized by the clergy in their counseling and religious interpretations.

Support for local clergy to address the sexual needs of older members was given in 1974 when the National Council of Churches, the Synagogue Council of America and the United States Catholic Conference issued an interfaith statement on sex education affirming that:

> human sexuality is a gift of God to be accepted with reverance and joy; . . . It is more than a mechanical instinct. Its many dimensions are intertwined with the total personality and character of the individual. Sex is a dynamic urge or power, arising from one's basic maleness or femaleness, and having complex physical, psychological, and sexual dimensions. These dimensions, we affirm, must be shaped and guided by spiritual and moral considerations which derive from our Judeo-Christian heritage. Sex education is not however, only for the young, but is a life-long task whose aim is to help individuals develop their sexuality in a manner suited to their life stage.[12]

Implications for the Church/Synagogue

As the age of the church/synagogue shifts from youth to an adult membership, sex after sixty will no longer be a laughing matter but the reason for life-span sex education and social programs to provide opportunities for heterosexual interaction.

The influence of the sheer numbers of the Baby Boomers and their sexual life styles will shape the future direction of these changes. The shift to an older adult membership will make it imperative to rely on retired members to fill the functional lay leader roles in the congregations. This age group, with the most discretionary time and income, will be a major source for recruitment and training for diaconal ministry. The youth-to-adult to older-adult congregations will require a trained lay older adult leadership to carry out the goals and programs for all age members.

FROM MALE TO FEMALE CONGREGATIONS

For fifty years the Gallup report on Religion in America has shown church/synagogue membership to be highest among women.[13] However, being in the majority did not constitute a female-oriented congregation. The women's movement and the increase in the number of older women have caused a shift from a male-dominated (and not majority) church/synagogue to one in which women are not only increasing in membership but also filling traditionally-held male lay and professional roles.

Longevity is not experienced equally by males and females. In 1984, life expectancy at birth for the male was 71.1 and for the female it was 78.3 years. For those reaching the age of 65, females had a life expectancy of 18.7 more years and men had an additional 14.5 years. This difference in life expectancy at birth and at age 65 results in a ratio of males to females which varies dramatically with age. Until the age of 24, there is only a slight difference in the numbers of males and females. After age 25, their sex ratio begins to change until by age 65 women outnumber men three to two. Among those over the age of 85 in 1984, there were 40 men for every 100 women or four women for every man.[14]

These sex differences in life expectancy result partly from sex differences in the cause of death. Women have benefited from medical advances in treating infectious diseases, pre-natal care and birth control. Men are more likely than women to die of degenerative diseases such as cancer and heart disease. Although there has been progress in treating these diseases, it has not been as great as for infectious diseases.[15] There is some speculation, supported by the slight increase in life expectancy for the male and decline for the female, that the mass entry of women, especially the Baby Boomers, into the work force may make women more vulnerable to the degenerative diseases that have contributed to the shorter life expectancy of the male. Others speculate that as the male is relieved of the financial stress as the sole financial support for the family he will be less vulnerable to degenerative diseases. This could narrow the life expectancy differential significantly by the year 2000.

The implication of this trend is that the sex-ratio disparity can be expected to be greater in the church/synagogues than in the general population. The sex ratio differential among the older age groups and the age differential between youth and adults will impact program emphases and leadership. These age-sex trends could result in: (1) a more intergenerational organizational structure or a polarity and conflict between the young and older adults; (2) either a high dropout rate among older men who are uncomfortable with the increased disproportionate number of men to women or their increased involvement in the church/synagogue because they have more discretionary time; and (3) the Baby Boomer women filling more lay and professional leadership roles in the church/synagogue.

Regardless of which of these alternatives are taken, the sex ratio disparity among older members will force some programmatic and leadership changes in the congregations.

FROM MARRIED TO SINGLE

Congregations have not only been youth and male oriented, but couple and family oriented. Congregations have been characterized by a "Noah's ark" syndrome in which all are expected to enter two by two. This Noah's ark syndrome is a sex-negativism that places primacy on sexual activity as procreation. Important as this aspect of sexuality is, it is age specific for women and does not represent the total experience of human sexuality.

The disparity of males to females among older adults means that there are fewer married couples. In 1984, 40 percent of adults age 65 and over were married. Twice as many older men (78%) were likely to be married than older women (40%). There were five times (7.8 million) widows as widowers (1.5 million) and the disparity increases at older ages.[16] In 1985, 68% of women 75 and older were widowed compared to less than 23% of men over age 75. This gender disparity is a consequence of age-specific death rates for adult men and their tendency to marry younger women.[17]

Divorce among older people has increased faster than the older population as a whole in the past 20 years. Four percent of all older persons were divorced — more older women than older men. Furthermore, elderly widowed men have remarriage rates about seven times higher than widows. Among the future elderly (men and women) approximately one-half of the men and women will have been divorced at least once by the time they reach the age of 75. [18] This may seem like a dismal projection, but on the positive side, they (men and women) will know how to enter and exit a single lifestyle. For women, this may be the best preparation for the eight to ten years most of them over the age of 65 can expect to be widowed or divorced.

A small number (less than 8%) of older persons never marry. Since many young adults are delaying or rejecting marriage, the number of never married older persons may be expected to increase. [19] Studies on marital status and life satisfaction are in general agreement that married persons are happier, healthier and longer-lived than the never-married, widowed or divorced. [20] Marriage minimizes the negative impact of retirement, reduced income and declining health. This life satisfaction difference may be attributed to the major functions that marriage performs for couples: intimacy, interdependence, a sense of belonging, a shared life history, and continuity of life style. [21]

Marital satisfaction varies among older couples, but most of the studies reported that older wives and husbands appreciate each other and are highly satisfied, whether it is a long- or short-term marriage. Given the personal investment of time, energy and themselves in the marriage and the alternative of living alone in late life, most dissatisfied older marrieds choose to continue the relationship. [22]

The church/synagogue is challenged to respond to never-married, widowed and divorced older members who also have the need to minimize the negative impact of retirement, reduced income and declining health.

Implications for the Church/Synagogue

Gender differences in marital status are much greater among older age groups and can be expected to continue. Responses to this marital heterogeneity by the church/synagogue will include: (1) older singles groups to provide social support and activities that increase morale and life satisfaction; (2) support groups for those experiencing loss of a spouse by divorce or death; (3) marital counseling and adaptation of the marriage ritual for late-life remarriages; (4) couple groups for the older newlyweds; and (5) marriage revitalization and enrichment groups for long-lived intact-survivor marriages.

All of these groups will need leaders, counselors and clergy who are knowledgeable about normal physiological aging and gender changes in sexual functionality.

FROM EITHER/OR TO MULTIPLE CHOICE

Marriage continues to be the most valued state for most Americans. At least 95% marry at least once and most who divorce before they are sixty tend to marry again. Although death and divorce reduce the numbers of older marriages, approximately half of the 26 million older Americans are married. Of course, this means that approximately half of these older Americans are not married and that the sex ratio disparity reduces the chances for remarriage, especially for women.

The opportunity for heterosexual activity on the part of the older female, unlike that of the older male or young female, is still more apt to be determined by the availability of a husband and his sexual capability. Unmarried older men maintain sexual activity and interest levels similar to that of married men. Women do not because they lack available and appropriate sexual partners.

The sexual revolution of the past two decades has widened the choices for adults of all ages. The trend has been away from sexual intimacy within marriage or to multiple choices. Although marriage continues to be highly valued by older persons and a life style experienced by most, it can no longer be the only alternative.

The choices other than marriage include: (1) companionship and dating; (2) co-habitation; (3) homosexuality; (4) affairs with married persons; (5) polygamy; and (6) no sexual partner.

Marriage and dating may be the only choices sanctioned by the church/synagogue. However, the sex ratio disparity among older persons can be expected to influence these limited sanctions in the future. Certainly, the Judeo-Christian faith has an Old Testament precedent for multiple partners. Courtship and dating may lead to marriage or to a "steady" relationship. Dating behavior among older persons is reported to be more varied and the pace of the relationship tends to be accelerated. Bulcroft and O'Conner-Roden report that sexual involvement is an important part of the dating relationships for most of the older persons in their study. While sexuality for these dating couples included intercourse, the stronger emphasis was on the nuances of sexual behavior, such as hugging, kissing and touching. This physical closeness helped fulfill the intimacy needs of older people, needs that were especially important to those living alone and whose sole source of human touch was often the dating partner. Sex also contributed to self-esteem by making people feel desired and needed. As could be expected, older persons choosing to have a sexual relationship outside of marriage violated the religious values that they have followed. Consequently, older people frequently hide the intimate aspects of a relationship. [23]

Some older persons elect to openly live together. For some this may lead to marriage. Many older people reject marriage as a solution to their need for a sexual relationship because they are not willing to give up their independence, the possibility of deteriorating health and the financial complexities of a legal relationship. Brubaker observes that although the number of people over the age of 65 cohabiting has decreased slightly, cohabitation is increasing in most age groups. [24] This leads us to expect the trend toward cohabitation to gradually increase. The choice of dating with intimacy and cohabitation raises the religious question about the reason for marriage. Do older people have the same reason for marriage as young people? Is the delay in marriage by young adults based on the same rationale that older people use to reject marriage, i.e., the view that marriage is for procreation? This ambiguity about marriage by both young and older adults may stimulate the church/synagogues to formulate sanctions and rituals that address age-related sexual expressions and relationships.

Another form of cohabitation is homosexual. The visibility of homosexuality among younger adults may lead older adults, especially older women, to choose this life style to meet their needs for intimacy. Unanswered is the effect of AIDS on the *number* of homosexuals in the future. However, it is most likely that a homosexual cohabitation will continue to be the choice of a small proportion of older persons.

Over forty years ago a medical doctor, Victor Kassells, recommended a limited polygamy after the age of 60. He pointed out that this would be a return to a practice that at one time was considered proper in the Judeo-Christian ethic. He argued that:

marriage enables the unmarried older women to find a partner. . . . Most women have an increase in libido after the meno-

pause simply because they lose the fear of pregnancy. A poly-
gynous marriage enables them to express this desire, instead
of remaining repressed through a continent widowhood.[25]

As for men, Kassells observed that many sexologists claim the
male is polygamous by nature. Furthermore, there is no established
age of a male climacteric. Male impotence, not related to disease or
medication, may be due to boredom, or an uninterested partner.
Polygamous marriage might be a solution to a number of sexual
problems of the aged. Kassells may have a good solution, but the
strength of the Christian belief in a monogamous relationship, at
least serially within and outside of marriage, makes it unlikely that
this choice will be sanctioned in the future.

More likely to increase are affairs outside of marriage. As partners within a long-term marriage experience changes in health, interests and compatibility, discrete affairs that protect the marriage
partners may be a choice for some older persons.

Always open as choice is no sexual partner. Many widowed persons find a new freedom without sexual relationships. They focus
their energy and interests on other activities and relationships. The
importance that Americans of all ages place on sex suggests that this
will not be the voluntary choice of most older adults in the future.

Implications for the Church/Synagogue

The need and requests for counseling related to these choices can
be expected to increase. Consequently, the professional training for
clergy and other counselors will include not only the sexual needs,
choices, sociopsychological problems unique to older persons, but
also the religious conflict and dilemma older persons experience.

Church/synagogue rituals related to marriage and sexual practice
will need to be adapted to the non-procreative stage of life so that
the joy of intimacy, experiencing one's sexuality and identity on
human sexuality will be extended to older members.

FROM EXCLUSION TO INCLUSION

This fifth trend is a logical consequence of the other trends discussed above. For the never married, widowed and divorced older
adult, the congregation has the opportunity to provide the many

opportunities for forms of sexual expression, such as caring, touching, hugging, kissing and dating. Congregations may also serve as a surrogate extended family. The exclusion of the unique problems of older married couples for marital counseling training will give way to an inclusion which views marriage within a life stage model. Younger and older persons will benefit from such inclusion.

The single older persons will be included in the singles ministry of the church/synagogue.

Sex education and premarital counseling will include age changes in sexual needs and interest and age appropriate counseling. Theological statements and rituals will be included and adapted at the congregational level to increase the human sexuality of older persons.

The inclusion of older persons in all religious matters related to sex, sex roles and sexuality will destroy the bases for making sex and the elderly a laughing matter.

NOTES

1. "Genesis," Chapter 17:17; 18:12-13. *The Holy Bible*, revised standard version (New York: Thomas Nelson and Sons, 1953), pp. 10-12.

2. Stagg, Frank. *The Bible Speaks on Aging* (Nashville, TN: Broadman Press, 1981).

3. Bulcroft, Kris & Margaret O'Connor-Roden. "Never Too Late," *Psychology Today*, June 1986, pp. 66-69; "Old Folks Who Fall in Love Still Teenagers at Heart," The Atlanta Journal/Constitution, May 29, 1986.

4. Beckner, Arthur H. *Ministry With Older Persons: A Guide for Clergy and Congregations* (Minneapolis: Augsberge Publishing House, 1986).

5. Payne, Barbara. "Religiosity." In Mangen, David J. & Warren A. Peterson (eds.), *Social Roles and Social Participation*, Vol. 2 (Minneapolis: University of Minnesota Press, 1983), pp. 343-388; Kechner, Vincent. *Religion and Aging: An Annotated Bibliography* (San Antonio, Texas, 1982).

6. Alston, Jon P. & Wingrove, Ray (eds.). "Cohort Analysis of Church Attendance, 1936-69." In *Social Forces*, 1949, September, pp. 59-17.

7. "The World is Not Just for the Young: Atlanta's Median Age is 31.1," The Atlanta Journal/Constitution, June, 1986.

8. *Aging America: Trends and Projections* (1985-86 edition) (Washington: U.S. Senate Special Committee on Aging), The American Association of Retired Persons, The Federal Council on Aging & The Administration on Aging, 1986.

9. Thoason, James A. & Horacek, Bruce S., "Self Esteem, Value, and Identity: Who are the Elderly Really?" *Journal of Religion and Aging*, 3(1/2): pp. 5-15.

10. Payne, Barbara. "Protestants." In Erdman Palmore (ed.), *Handbook on the Aged in the United States* (Westport, Connecticut, 1984) pp. 181-198.

11. Palmore, Erdman. "Sexual Behavior." In *Social Patterns in Normal Aging: Findings from the Duke Longitudinal Study* (Durham, North Carolina: Duke University Press, 1981); Butler, Robert & Lewis, Myra, *Sex After Sixty* (New York: Harper & Row, 1976; Peterson, James A. & Payne, Barbara, *Love in the Later Years* (Association Press, 1975).

12. "Interfaith Statement on Sex Education" (National Council of Churches, Synagogue Council of America, United States Catholic Council). In Gordon, S. & Libby, R. *Sexuality Today and Tomorrow* (North Scituate, Mass: Duxbury Press, 1976), pp. 154-156.

13. Gallup, Jr., George, *Religion in America. 50 years: 1935-1985* (Princeton, NJ: Gallup Report, N0236, May 1985).

14. *Aging America: Trends and Projections* (1985-86 edition). (Washington D.C.: U.S. Senate Committee on Aging, The American Association of Retired Persons, The Federal Council on Aging and The Administration on Aging, 1986.

15. Ward, Russell A., *The Aging Experience* (second ed.) (New York: Harper & Row, Publishers; 1984); pp. 207-209.

16. Glick, Paul C. "Marriage, Divorce and Living Arrangements of the Elderly: Prospective Changes," *Journal of Family Issues* 5:7-26, 1984.

17. "Developments in Aging: 1985," Volume 3 (Washington, D.C.: Special Committee on Aging, United States Senate, 1986).

18. Brubaker, Timothy. *Later Life Families* (Beverly Hills, California: Sage, 1985).

19. *Psychology Today* (see footnote #3).

20. Ward, Russell A. "The Never Married In Later Life," *Journal of Gerontology* 34:861-869, 1979. Gubrium, Jay F., "Being Single in Old Age," *International Journal of Aging and Human Development* 6:29-41, 1975; Longino, Jr., Charles F. & Lipman Aaron, "The Married, The Formerly Married and The Never Married: Support System Differentials of Older Women in Planned Retirement Communities," 1982; Norvel, Glenn, "The Contribution of Marriage to the Psychological Well-being of Males and Females." *Journal of Marriage and the Family* 37(3):594-601; Brubaker, 113-116 (see footnote #18); Uhlenberg, P. & Myers, M. "Divorce and The Elderly" *Gerontologist* 21(3), 276-82, 1981.

21. Atchley, Robert. *Social Forces and Aging* (4th ed.) (Belmont, California: Wadsworth, 1985).

22. Gilford, Rosalie. "Marriages in Later Life," *Generations* X(4):17-21, 1986; Skolink, A., "Married Lives: Longitudinal Perspectives on Marriage." In Eichorn, David et al. (eds.) *Present and Past in Middle Life* (New York: Academic Press, 1981).

23. Bulcroft, Kris, and O'Connor-Roden, Margaret (see footnote #3).

24. Brubaker, Timothy (see Footnote #18).

25. Kassels, Victor. "Polygamy After 60," *Geriatrics* 21, No. 4, April 1966.

The *Real* Nursing Home Scandal: Will It Get Worse in the Future?

David B. Oliver, PhD

SUMMARY. The primary support system for older persons is and always has been the family. In the 21st century, however, the config-uration of the average American family will continue to change, making it less responsive to the needs of older members. Will the church/synagogue/parish fill the gap and become the extended fam-ily for disconnected and isolated older persons, particularly for those who will be living in nursing homes? While nursing homes are criti-cized for what is sometimes described as deplorable conditions and poor quality care, this blame is often misplaced. It is the religious sector which has abandoned those who live in nursing homes. Will this trend become worse, or get better?

A sense of belonging, of participating, of being part of some sort of intimate group brings drama to life. This is perhaps most pro-nounced and experienced in close interpersonal relationships — in social bonds which connect us to our dearest and closest friends. The pain, agony and despair which we all feel with the loss of one of these relationships (be it through death, divorce, geographical displacement, ill health, etc.) is sufficient evidence to remind us of the importance of our having been membered to the person. Friend-ship is a powerful force. It begins early in life, and without it, the human species suffers immeasurably.

For most older persons the loss of close friends and relatives is synonymous with the aging process — the longer persons live, the greater the likelihood they will be abandoned to face life alone. It

---

David B. Oliver is Professor of and holds the Oubri A. Popple Chair in Gerontology and Health and Welfare Studies at Saint Paul School of Theology, Kansas City, Missouri.

becomes especially difficult when the closest of friends, our confidants, die. There is perhaps nothing more devastating about growing older than having no one with whom to share our secrets. When no one will listen to our story, or worse, when they only pretend to listen, we begin a psychological death which can long precede the physical one.

Abandonment in old age is most clearly evident for persons who live in nursing homes. Teaching my classes on "The World of Nursing Homes" in long-term care facilities (for fifteen years now) exposes the realities of this disconnectedness from life. Students and myself spend long hours in wheelchairs, gerichairs, eat pureed food, and even, on occasion, spend 24 hours (overnight) in the institutions. One sees the world of the nursing home from a different perspective when the role of the resident is assumed. We experience moments of tender loving care, the sharing of compassion, the experience of pain and loss, the humor of daily living, and overall, a drama of life which is played out on a stage which cannot be found in any other setting. It is a place in which real humanness exists. Societal pretense, synthetic smiles, and fabricated faces won't work here. To visit a nursing home means to face life as it really is, on its own terms. For most Americans, visiting there is threatening. The response is often the putting on of blinders, so that they will not have to confront the realities which surround them.

Every time I read about some kind of nursing home scandal, or read a government report criticizing the quality of care provided in homes, or overhear a family member, student, clergyperson, or other, wax righteously over the deplorable conditions of nursing homes in general, and/or a local home in particular, I get sick to my stomach. This feeling is more intense when I hear members of a church/synagogue/parish carry on in the same fashion. This aggression, often produced out of personal guilt, is misplaced. There are no enemies here, only ourselves. If there is a problem with nursing homes in America, it rests at the societal and personal level, not at the local organizational level. What bothers people most about nursing homes is the perceived extent to which the people living there are treated. And how are they treated? They are denied the most important thing which makes life a drama. They are denied our continued fellowship, friendship, and continued encounters which make life the exciting enterprise that it is. We are the problem, but we put the blame elsewhere.

It hurts to hear a nursing home resident tell how they were a member of a particular religious community for so many years only to be abandoned by that same community upon entering the nursing home. Ministers themselves acknowledge this tendency toward withdrawal. In a study of graduates from a major theological seminary, the most-reported problem relating to ministry with older persons is the guilt felt by the pastors for not visiting more often in nursing homes. Despite the rhetoric, it remains to be seen if the church/synagogue/parish can become the extended family for older persons in America.

FAMILY AS CAREGIVER

The family is and always has been the primary support group for older persons. It provides financial, social and emotional resources for celebrating and healing, it provides a sense of belonging and a sense of transcending, and it usually is made up of persons who will, whether out of duty or love, stay loyally close as life comes to an end for one of its members. Many of life's memories are family-related.

Some years ago, my wife and I were travelling across Missouri on a summer vacation. We stopped at a restaurant along the interstate for a delightful meal. The dining area was comfortably complete with tablecloths, soft light, some music and an appealing decor — not bad for a highway respite. On one side of us was seated an elderly couple, and on the other side was a young couple. The young man and woman were clearly on their honeymoon. The older persons finished their meal first and went on their way. Ten minutes later my wife and I, and the honeymooners, got up to leave at the same time. As the young groom tried to pay for the meal, the receptionist said, "Are you and your wife just married?"

"Yes, we were married this morning," the man replied both proudly and with some nervousness.

"I thought so; your bill has been paid," she told them.

"Paid? What do you mean paid?" asked the young man.

"It was the elderly couple sitting across from you. Didn't you see them? They guessed you were on your honeymoon and wanted to add to your celebration by paying your bill," the receptionist explained.

"Where are they?" the young bride asked as she looked about the room. "We want to thank them!"

"Oh, they left some time ago," the lady replied. "They must be miles down the road by now."

Only an older couple, who have been where the honeymooners are going, could fully appreciate the rite of passage unfolding before their eyes. Memories are special, and they are particularly meaningful when they can be seen repeated in the lives of others. Intimate social relationships make life a drama.

Yet while the family remains the most important social and sacred unit, its role as the primary support system is changing. And in the next fifty years, it will change even more.

At the turn of the century (1900), the average number of children per American family was four.[1] It was not, however, unusual for many families to have eight, nine, or even ten offspring (my grandmother is one of twelve children). Large families usually meant that someone would be left over to take care of mother and/or father — and this responsibility was expected of daughters more often than of sons (in fact, geriatric care in the United States could be spelled W-O-M-A-N). Daughters, daughters-in-law and sisters were (and are) often called when special care was (is) needed. In short, it was the women who took care of the older members. Nursing homes, for the most part, did not exist.

As we move into the 21st century (2000), the family statistics will continue to change in a very different direction. There are now two persons born per American couple instead of four.[2] So at the outset, the potential pool of caregivers is limited. The women, the primary caregivers of the past, are not at home. Nearly three out of four between the ages of 45 and 64 are in the labor force working full-time.[3] It is not easy to care for mother and/or dad when you work all day. And to complicate matters, one out of two first marriages now end in divorce. This further weakens the support system for those who will live into old age.

To make the situation yet more grim, the average number of persons living in households (for all ages) is less than three.[4] For older persons it is, of course, even less. This trend does not appear to be reversing. By the time the Baby Boomers reach old age (in less than twenty-five years), one must wonder who in the world is going to provide support for them. Nursing home statistics and projections suggest one answer to the question.

Prior to the Medicare and Medicaid legislation (in the mid-sixties), there were approximately 400,000 nursing home beds in America. By the early '70s, this figure doubled. And currently there are approximately 1.5 million beds which exceeds the number of acute care hospital beds. Future projections are staggering.

By the year 2000, the number of nursing home beds will increase to 2.2 million (an 80 percent increase over 1980), and by 2020, we will have 3.0 million beds. For those looking into the distant future, it is projected that 5.4 million beds will be filled in the year 2050 (a whopping 300 percent increase over 1980).[5] Much of this growth is accounted for by the increasing number of persons who are living to their full potential life expectancy. The 85 and over age group in America is the fastest growing cohort. Indeed, by the year 2050, two-thirds of all nursing home residents will be in this age category.[6]

All this is particularly relevant for religious professionals, for religious communities and for religious persons. The traditional image of the church/synagogue/parish as "family" is professed as the doctrine of most religious people. While this concept is preached, it is not always practiced. When one ponders the alarming statistic that nearly 60% of nursing home residents don't get a single visit from an outsider during the course of the year,[7] one should be cautious about singing praises of how effective their "family" is in ministry with older persons.

Ironically, in the last 100 years, "religion" has been taken *out* of the family and put into a free-standing building. The 64 dollar question is whether or not the "family" can follow religion into the building. Will religious communities become the extended families for those who are losing and who have lost their primary support system? If not, there may be little to attract the Baby Boomers back to the church/synagogue/parish. Too many are already seeing their parents and grandparents being abandoned by the religious community when they (the elders) can no longer participate in it as fully active and "productive" members.

Even within the church/synagogue/parish itself, older persons are often isolated and age-segregated from other age groups. This is rarely intentional, but seemingly it is the way people think it ought to be. We retire people in the larger society, and we retire them in the community of faith as well. It is scary to contemplate a future which finds the church/synagogue/parish much like many small towns in America. Will the religious community cease to exist as the younger people leave the community and the older people die off?

CHURCH/SYNAGOGUE/PARISH AS CAREGIVER

It should be stated that most religious communities do have persons who visit regularly in nursing homes. And some of these persons visit not only members of their own church/synagogue/parish, but also other residents in the home. Unfortunately, these individuals are few and far between. In the future we will need to call upon these experienced lovers for advice and counsel on how to get past the wrinkles and see the person. They are the experts; few others have been there.

Most of the contact with religious communities is imported from the outside. Few nursing homes have full-time chaplains (perhaps less than 10%), but most have a list of volunteers who bring a worship service to the home on a regular basis. Frequently, however, the volunteer (often a professional minister, rabbi or priest) is anxious to be finished and on his or her way. The message does not always relate to the life-world in which the residents find themselves, nor does it reach a large number of persons. If a sufficient number of persons from the church/synagogue/parish were regularly in the home (at least one person every day), possibilities for developing a community of faith from within the home would be better. What is needed is a caring community of residents who minister to each other and to those who visit from the outside.

In short, if I ever end up in a nursing home, I want to have a support group within the home. Alcoholics have support groups, relatives and friends of Alzheimer's Disease patients have support groups, retirement communities have support groups — why can't I have a support group as a nursing home resident? What is needed, of course, is a common bond. Since 95% of older persons have a strong faith in a power greater than themselves, perhaps it will be my faith which will offer the rallying point. It seems so natural. But where is the church/synagogue/parish? Will it respond? Why is the nursing home treated like a leper colony?

Images of aging must first be overcome for any significant shift to occur. What we have here is an attitude problem. Future efforts to connect long-term health care with religious communities will require a new conceptualization of aging. Value and worth lie beneath the worn-out body, but how do we get past the wrinkles and say, "Hello, in there." A stroke patient can teach us grace and acceptance, but how do we say, "It's nice just being here with you." We will change the diaper of a six-month-old child with little resistance, but if asked to clean up after a 90-year-old whose bottom is soiled, we avoid it at all costs. How do we say, "Let me wash your feet and body"? If our dear relative forgets our name, how can we say, "Why my name is David" (and not worry about it)? When we are told that, "Nobody loves me anymore," how can we reply, "But I do" (and mean it)? If we have to yell loud in order to be heard and to be understood, how do we do so without embarrassment?

The church/synagogue/parish needs to move its people beyond superficial pretense and game-playing. Honesty and acceptance of persons — unconditionally — must be a goal. I am fascinated by many staff persons in nursing homes. They are good role models. They know that when dealing, say, with an Alzheimer's patient, who can no longer wear a mask (a synthetic smile or a fabricated face), what is often left is humanness in all its glory. They learn to accept it, appreciate it and miss it when the patient dies. The rest of us avoid it, deny it, and cry about it.

Perhaps the biggest problem is the fact that a majority of Americans, mostly younger, fail to realize that none of us gets out of this alive. All living things die. There is a tree in the Middle East that lives nearly 7,000 years, but eventually it dies too. Our pets die, the flowers die, every living thing dies. This clearly calls for a theology of death. I would like to think it is all part of the Creation, at least that is more comforting to me. Others make other claims. An examination of these views seems worthy of discussion. In the future, the Baby Boomers may want an alternative to the notion that the "wages of sin are death." My experience with many older persons would suggest the same thing.

THE FUTURE

If I am to continue to feel membered to a religious community, to feel loved, as if somehow I count, that I'm still somebody, then a number of things need to happen between now and 33 years from now when I will be a prime candidate for a nursing home. Although I may feel differently when I am 77 years of age, I will represent a new generation characterized by its own history and set of expectations. Each day now, approximately 5500 birthdays are celebrated by persons who have reached their 65th year. Funerals are performed each day for approximately 4000 persons who are age 65 or older.[8] Thus with each passing 24 hours, nearly 1550 new persons join the 65-and-older cohort in the United States. By the time I become one of this group, my wants and desires will reflect my own history and experiences along the life-course. I can predict, I think with some accuracy, that I will want the following:

1. I hope that someone will be around with whom I can share stories. Every time we listen to stories, we accord the other value and worth. I don't want people to pretend to listen, and I don't want them to be in a hurry. I want them to interiorize me with respect, and I will try to do the same with them. Perhaps we can make an agreement not to tell the same stories during the same day. If others ask me for advice (after all, I will have been where most of them are going), that will be especially rewarding. Given the limited resources and time of the nursing home staff, I hope a volunteer, or someone, visits me regularly from my church/synagogue/parish. Several times each week will be fine.

2. I want an Ethics Committee to have been established in my nursing home. If possible, I want death to come on my terms. The right to die with dignity is very important. Hopefully my religious affiliation will support such an enterprise and contribute theological understandings to it. Perhaps they will call on me to provide input and wisdom. They will if they value my experience and long years of relating to God, my confidant.

3. I expect the bill to be paid. If this is out of my own pocket, fine. I fully expect to be receiving a good pension, social security (or its equivalent), private health insurance benefits (which by then will cover chronic health conditions and long term health care); and the sale of my home (which should be paid for by then) will enhance any savings I have accumulated. Collectively this should pool enough money to cover expenses. If, however, I have lost a good bit or all of these resources, I fully expect the bill to be paid anyway. I expect a national health insurance plan (a form of socialized medicine similar to the European plans) to have been adopted by the year 2019 to assist the poor in long-term care living. Health care will hopefully become a right, not a privilege. I will, of course, be lucky. I will most likely be living in a nice middle-class home supported with pride by my religious affiliation. I hope by then my religious group has decided to put its name on homes for the poor as well.

4. I want the home to accept my unique personality and special interests. After all, we become different from each other the longer and longer we live. If there are 30 people living on my unit, I want the activity programmer to have at least 30 alternative activities planned. This means they will have to do a careful inventory of my likes and dislikes. They will not, of course, be able to provide 30 programs on my floor. People in my church/synagogue/parish, however, should already know my likes and dislikes and will look after me regularly. Or will they?

5. I don't want to be entertained all the time. And I certainly hope everyone isn't trying to make me happy all the time. I want to serve others, be in missions in whatever ways possible. Hopefully it will be a requirement of the nursing home I enter. That would show real progress. Hopefully my church/synagogue/parish will expect me to continue my servanthood (I know they will appreciate my continued financial stewardship). If they get me a phone I could always participate (even organize if I have the energy) a telephone reassurance program for my church/synagogue/parish. You know it will be a sin, by then, if this is not going on in my community of faith.

6. I want to be connected to a worshipping, caring community within the nursing home. And from time to time, I want to visit my old religious home (church/synagogue/parish). Hopefully it will not look foreign to me, for I expect to receive regular visits from a number and variety of persons in the congregation. If this is not the case, the future role of the religious sector looks bleak indeed.

7. Oh, yes, I want a jacuzzi, a VCR, and a motorized wheelchair. I will also accept any innovative games and activities devised especially for nursing home residents. If the home cannot provide these luxuries, surely my church/synagogue/parish will. After all, don't we do all we can for our family members?

8. Transportation out of the home is critical. By 2019, there will surely be all kinds of ways to transport persons with challenging conditions. I want to go for rides even if everyone on my floor thinks I'm out of it. When was the last time you went to a nursing home and took someone for a ride?

9. Give me space. Everyone knows what happens in a rat cage when the cage becomes overcrowded. I don't mind having a roommate, but I want more than a curtain between our lives. I fully expect architecture and architects to be enlightened by

the year 2019. Personal space and social (living) space should be adequate for the formation of acquaintances and close friends. I want to decide on my own terms which will be which. I will particularly like going for rides in my wheelchair in the local parks. I hope someone will take me.

10. I want to stay politically involved and socially aware. Bring in outsiders to state their positions, and take me into the larger world to take a stand. By 2019, the Baby Boomers will be fully realizing their potential as a powerful political force. They will want me to help. The good news is that they will probably accept me. I can always show up in my wheelchair to take my stand.

The degree to which the church/synagogue/parish gets involved in reconnecting nursing home residents to the larger body of believers remains to be seen. The kind of expectations listed here, however, represent a generational attitude which carries over to the religious sector as well. If the church/synagogue/parish fails to respond, it may very well find itself as playing a minor role in future societal affairs.

CONNECTED OR NOT?

It is my view that the way in which religious communities respond to the isolation and disconnectedness of people in nursing homes is a good measure of their claim to be a community of faith. In fact, if any member of a congregation fails to receive a regular visit from other members of the congregation, then that religious body should be held suspect. Unfortunately, I am aware of a congregational member of a large California church who used to attend, with his wheelchair-restricted wife, the regular Sunday School Older Adults Class. When members of the class complained to the minister about the wife's drooling and the smell from the tube containing her pee, he asked the man to discontinue bringing his wife to the class. Perhaps, in some communities, they are cut off even before the removal by natural means.

The *real* scandal surrounding nursing homes is the abandonment of them by the larger society in general, and by religious communities in particular. Criticisms are legitimate if addressed to Congress and to others who appropriate funds to enhance the quality of life in old age. But if they are addressed to the local nursing home, one should examine first his or her own involvement and ministry in these settings. When was the last time you spent a full day in a nursing home? How many days (hours?) each year do you spend there? Each month? Each week?

Now let me come clean. I may teach my classes on nursing homes *in* nursing homes, and I may advocate greater responsibility on the part of the religious sector, but I don't visit Dawson often enough. You see he is a member of my community of faith. I drive home each day and can look just beyond the interstate and see the nursing home in which he lives. I think about visiting him often, but I don't. You see, I too am a member of a congregation which often fails its older members. I may preach a solution, but, alas, I am part of the problem. My "religious family" is less membered to its parts than most, and I have done little to improve it. I suppose what I want for older persons is basically what I want for myself. There is work to be done.

NOTES

1. Special Committee on Aging, United States Senate, *America in Transition: An Aging Society*, 1984-85 Edition, Serial No. 99-B, June, 1985, p. 17.

2. *Ibid.*

3. *Ibid.*, p. 61.

4. U.S. Bureau of the Census, *Mid-Year Report*, March, 1985.

5. Special Committee on Aging, United States Senate, *America in Transition*, U.S. Government Printing Office, 1984.

6. *Ibid.*

7. Frank E. Moss & Val J. Halamandaris. *Too Old, Too Sick, Too Bad: Nursing Homes in America* (Germantown, Maryland: Aspen Systems Corporation, 1977), p. 8.

8. *A Profile of Older Americans: 1985*. Program Resources Department, American Association of Retired Persons, 1909 K Street, N.W., Washington, D.C. 20049.

Suicide Among the Elderly: The Religious Response

Rabbi Edward Paul Cohn, DMin

SUMMARY. This is an article which shares one rabbi's research and reflections on the subject of suicide among the elderly. Remembering one such instance which occurred early on in his training for the rabbinate, three questions are addressed: What are some of the recent findings regarding incidence and reasons for such suicides; What has been the Judeo-Christian attitude toward suicide throughout the centuries and up until the present day; and finally, What future steps will be necessary if the religious community is to respond worthily to the challenge of elderly suicides? From a futurist perspective, how might theological training and congregational-parish life reflect a determined effort to lessen the number of elderly suicides?

The voice on the phone informed me that they don't dig graves during the winter months in northern Michigan. Therefore, Bonnie R.'s funeral would have to be postponed for three months until the spring thaw arrived. Even though I was only a second year seminary student, I was Bonnie's rabbi and the family insisted that she would have wanted me to conduct her service.

We had only met the summer before while I served as the student rabbi for this small Michigan congregation whose formal religious services ended with the fall High Holy Days. Commuting became too difficult with the onset of winter weather.

Bonnie was a short, wiry woman in her early 60's, whose husband died following a long battle with heart disease shortly after my

Edward Paul Cohn is the rabbi of Temple Sinai, 5505 Forbes Avenue, Pittsburgh, Pennsylvania. He has a BA Degree from the University of Cincinnati (1970), Master of Hebrew Letters from Hebrew Union College – Jewish Institute of Religion (1974), and a Doctor of Ministry Degree from The St. Paul School of Theology of Kansas City, Missouri (1983).

arrival. Throughout my eight week stay with the Temple, Bonnie and her family turned to their rabbi for comfort and for guidance. The children, who were grown and married, naturally returned to their own homes before too long. Bonnie was left alone now. We saw one another frequently, engaging in many long and heavy conversations as she poured out her grief and intense loneliness. How would she cope? What meaning was left to her life? Why should she even go on? All of these and more were weighing her down.

As September approached, I visited Bonnie one last time before returning to my studies. She sat curled up in her favorite chair, wearing that same long shirt to which she had so taken as a security blanket. She tearfully assured me that, yes, she had listened to me and, yes, she would make a sincere effort to rebuild her world. Six months later, Bonnie took her life. And that was this rabbi's introduction to the phenomenon of suicide among the aged.

Naturally, many questions were raised in my mind, along with so many "What if's." Throughout the succeeding four years of theological study and a dozen years in the active congregational rabbinate, my mind has often turned to that small Michigan town on Lake Huron and to those conversations with Bonnie R. Often, I wonder to myself:

1. What would I know now that I didn't then?
2. What should we in the religious community recognize and consider vis-à-vis the subject of suicide among the elderly?
3. And finally, what must be the religious agenda in future years? What must be done for others like Bonnie who, for various reasons, conclude that their lives are no longer worth living?

These are the questions which I would now briefly address:

WHAT WOULD I KNOW NOW?

Some Current Statistics and Theories on Elderly Suicide

In her work, *Suicide in the Elderly*, Nancy Osgood confirms that:

> Suicide rates for different age groups suggest that suicide in the United States, and in most other industrialized countries

for which data are available, is clearly more frequent among older than younger persons.[1]

And although she believes that the oft-cited statistic that the aged, who account for but 10% of the population, commit 25% of the suicides is somewhat exaggerated, Osgood persists in supporting the view that maintains a positive relationship between age and suicide.[2]

Studies reveal that peak suicide rate occurs among white males in their eighties.[3] Specifically for men in their mid-eighties, the suicide rate is five times that of the general population.[4] Moreover, we also know that the incidence of suicide among the elderly is increased among widows and widowers and those living alone, and by the occurrence of wedding anniversaries, decline of health, physical change, or by those experiencing lowered social and economic status.[5]

Among those sixty years of age and older, physical sickness has been consistently cited as the most common precipitating factor in suicide.[6] The elderly are the ones most susceptible to painful, chronic and debilitating diseases such as cancer, Parkinson's disease, arthritis, heart disease and stroke. It does not take much insight to imagine how destructive an impact such disabilities may have upon any person up in years who may already be overwhelmed by the stress of loneliness, bereavement, or economic uncertainty. Osgood concludes that:

> Among the consequences of such disease are pain and suffering, body disfigurement, anxiety, worry, depression, loss of self-esteem and self-confidence, interruption of significant life activities and altered inter-personal relationships with "significant others."[7]

Thus, as pre-existent fears and concerns about infirmity, suffering and death grow real with the onset of illness, suicide is often seen as the aged person's way out. Research data have revealed that 15% of all persons aged sixty-five and older suffer from depression, a rate which dramatically climbs to 50% when extended to those elderly who are in poor health.

Perhaps due to our national preoccupation with youth and youthfulness, the headlines of late have drawn attention to the tragic incidence of teen suicide, but suicide among the elderly clearly poses a major social problem which needs to be addressed. Dr. Osgood cites several studies which have demonstrated that, unlike younger individuals, most of the aged who attempt suicide are deadly serious and intent on killing themselves.[9] Theirs is neither a cry for help nor a desperate attempt to gain attention, and the ratio of completed suicides to attempted suicides for the elderly is approximately 8:1. Moreover, numerous studies confirm that the elderly, with few exceptions, *do* succeed in their attempts at suicide.[10] And such studies explain this fact by pointing out that the elderly tend to use more lethal means of suicide and also possess far less innate physical strength.[11]

Osgood's most valuable new work on the subject of suicide among the elderly was ten years in the making. It began in 1975, while she was serving as a research fellow at Hutchings Psychiatric Center in Syracuse, New York.

> . . . I was involved in a purely academic study of suicide. The task was to examine the records of the county coroner in order to gather descriptive statistics on the number of suicides by age and sex. At some point during the study, while reading the suicide notes of different individuals of varying ages, it became apparent that many of the victims were over sixty, and that many of them had lost all hope for a happy, meaningful existence. I was impressed with the magnitude of the problem of elderly suicide, as well as with some of the reasons offered by those elderly individuals who chose to take their own lives. . . . The picture that emerged from the myriad of notes was not a pretty one.[12]

In addition to those contributing factors listed earlier, three others have been related to the high incidence of elderly suicide: change of residence, fear of institutionalization and dependency, and the status or value assigned to age by any given society.[13] In a recent address, one observer proffered this intriguing analysis.

> As cultures become less traditional, when age is no longer seen as a pathway to wisdom, when extended families fly to the wind, when people are considered interchangeable parts, when progress is highly valued, the suicide rates of the elderly will rise.[14]

I believe that the recent appearance of the popular film "Cocoon" only lends credence to this hypothesis. While joining the audience in giggling with delight at the notion of oldsters break-dancing and renewed in their vitality due to their swim with those extra-terrestrial pods, I also found the whole experience somewhat sobering. What a pathetic message it was that this crew of pre-senile men and women were called to choose between being "born-again" on an alien planet or remaining earthbound, only to become a burden to the younger members of *productive* society.

If it is true, as Emile Durkheim theorized in 1897,[15] that the nature and extent of one's involvement in society becomes a decisive factor in the incidence of suicide, then who should feign surprise by today's statistics of 5,000 to 8,000 elderly suicides per year in America alone? In a cultural milieu which continually pitches denture creams, figure salons, and a multi-billion dollar a year cosmetic industry to "make you feel young and look young again," just how much self-esteem is left for the aged?

One scholar aptly points out that unlike every other stage in the life cycle, the arrival of old age is accompanied by systematic status *loss*.

> All other statuses, from childhood through adolescence, to full maturity, are normally marked by steady social acquisitions of power, prestige and rewards. When people enter the latter stages of life and assume the aged role, however, for the first time loss of status is experienced. They now realize that the life goals they set for themselves may never be attained as the resources for achieving them dwindle before their eyes. [16]

Old age has often been referred to as the season of losses — emotional, psychological, physical, social and financial. Ample research and solid statistical data have provided unassailable evidence that the elderly represent a suicide-prone population. Out of their "insufferable anguish," as Herman Melville labels the psychological state of the suicide-prone in *Moby Dick*, the elderly have every right to expect that the religious community will be prepared to offer them some spiritual prophylaxis for their pain. The problem is, of course, that both as Jews and as Christians, more often than not, we have been found wanting.

THE RELIGIOUS COMMUNITY
AND THE ELDERLY SUICIDE

What Must We Recognize and Consider?

Within Jewish tradition, neither the Bible nor the Talmud articulate any laws against suicide, nor do they brand suicide as a sin. In fact, the earliest pronouncement on the "crime" of suicide is to be found in *Semachot*, a post-Talmudic work. Herein one learns that those who commit suicide are to receive no burial rites.

> He who destroys himself consciously, we do not engage ourselves with his funeral in any way. We do not tear the garments, and we do not bare the shoulder in mourning, and we do not say eulogies for him, . . . [17]

Also included in this treatise, *Semachot*, is the definition of suicide:

> . . . if a man is found hanged or fallen from a tree or a wall, he is not to be deemed a suicide unless he says "I am going to do so," and they see him climb up, . . . [18]

Notice that *only* the one who commits suicide with a clear mind and a predisclosed intention is to be considered a suicide. Jewish tradition has always been loath to declare suicide and has been mindful of mitigating stresses and circumstances which would make such actions understandable. If King Saul took his life, rather than be subjected to unspeakable torture, then tradition accounts the same right to a condemned prisoner who takes his own life in his cell while awaiting his execution.[19] Scholar Yechiel Epstein, in his late code, *Aruch Hashilchan*, 345, summarized the traditional Jewish attitude toward suicide in these words:

> We seek all sorts of reasons possible to explain away the man's actions, either his fear, or his pain, or temporary insanity, in order not to declare the man a suicide.

Clearly, since the criteria for determining a suicide within Jewish law were so stringent, whereby one would literally have to announce one's intention and then immediately fulfill it, there were many cases of *presumed* suicide, but apparently very few instances which were stigmatized as certainties. Ultimately, precedence is given to the feelings and dignity of the living within Jewish tradition. But having said this, let us recognize that the thrust of Jewish teaching throughout the ages has been upon the primacy of life and *Peku-ach Nefesh*, the saving of human life. This value would underscore the necessity of maintaining one's life and struggle until God, the Creator of all life, caused that soul to return "Home." The Talmudic dictum in Sanhedrin 4:45, "If a person saves a single life, it is as if he has saved the whole world," would presumably extend to self-preservation and to one's self-persistence with living life to the very end.

Interestingly, according to Professor William E. Phipps, in early Christianity suicide was sometimes considered a meritorious act. In his own account of the martyrs at Antioch, Eusebius even tells of a mother who taught her own virginal daughters that suicide was preferable to rape.[20] However, by the fourth century, Augustine limited the parameters of permissible suicide to those instances when one is "ordered by God."[21]

Aquinas later provided three arguments why suicide was to be viewed as a sin against self, neighbor and God. First, because it is contrary to nature. Second, said Aquinas, suicide is contrary to the Christian's social obligations. And third, because it is contrary to God's own right to decide the hour of life or death. Therefore, Aquinas continued:

To bring death upon oneself in order to escape other afflictions of this life is to adopt a greater evil in order to avoid a less . . . Suicide is the most fatal of sins because it cannot be repented of.[22]

Is there any wonder that the poet Dante, mindful of Aquinas' teachings, assigned those who took their own lives to the seventh level of hell, below the greedy and those who had murdered.

In the present century, the great Lutheran theologian and exemplar of faith amid extremis, Dietrich Bonhoeffer, seemed to follow in the tradition of Augustine insofar as suicide is concerned. Despite his own imprisonment, torture and eventual execution at the hands of the Nazis, Bonhoeffer insisted:

Even if a person's earthly life has become a torment for him, he must commit it intact to God's hand, from which it came.[24]

Dr. William Phipps, in his recent article, "Christian Perspectives on Suicide," draws what for some will be a rather startling conclusion:

> An examination of our Biblical and church heritage discloses different degrees of tolerance toward suicide. For some it is always absolutely wrong; for others it may be an appropriate response in exceptional situations. The historical discussion provides some guidance for facing current dilemmas. Modern medicine occasionally extends artificially the time of death — a fact that has generated fresh inquiry into situations in which suicide might be acceptable.[25]

Let us direct our attention now to the specific issue of the religious view of suicide among the elderly. Given the well-known statistics, we can now state with certainty that the most suicide-prone segment of our population is the elderly, many of whom are physically sick. No doubt a major explanation for this higher suicide rate in industrially sophisticated nations is the higher life expectancy these countries have afforded, and the larger percent of the total population in the elderly group. Many of these elderly clearly do *not* consider the quality of their lives to be worth the pain and effort it takes to go on.

A 78-year-old man suffering from multiple physical infirmities and facing major surgery pleaded with his physician to let him die a natural death rather than resorting to heroic means of life-support. Lacking any cooperation from these professionals, and following the initiation of forced feeding and dependence upon a respirator, this man finally reached over and switched off the life-support machine. They discovered this suicide note on the table beside his bed: "Death is not the enemy, doctor. Inhumanity is."[26]

Margaret Battin, who has addressed herself to the ethical issues in suicide, went so far at a 1981 Concern for Dying conference as to envision "A time in the distant future when Christians would come to treat suicide as a kind of sacrament involving a serious grappling with ultimate questions."[27]

The much-publicized double suicide of Dr. Henry Pitney Van Dusen and his wife Elizabeth at ages 77 and 80, respectively, has also engendered much discussion as to whether or not there are situations in which profoundly religious people might come to accept suicide as a conscientious and sane act resulting from a thorough consideration of the alternatives. Henry Van Dusen was the former president of the prestigious Union Theological Seminary in New York, as well as being a distinguished Presbyterian minister in his own right. Before taking their overdose of sleeping pills, Elizabeth Van Dusen left the following note:

> We have both had very full and satisfying lives . . . But
> . . . we have not been able to do any of the things we want to
> do . . . There are many helpless old people who without mod-
> ern medical care would have died, and we feel God would
> have allowed them to die when their time had come. Nowa-
> days it is difficult to die. We feel that this way we are taking
> will become more usual and acceptable as the years pass. We
> are both increasingly weak and unwell, and who would want
> to die in a nursing home? . . . "O Lord of God that takest
> away the sins of the world, grant us thy peace."[28]

Surely then, within the Judeo-Christian tradition, there are wide-ly varying degrees of tolerance toward suicide. For some religious thinkers, the very act of suicide is an inherent wrong and a mortal sin, while for others, in certain exceptional situations, suicide be-comes viewed as an appropriate option. From Aquinas' unwavering condemnation of all suicides, and the Talmudic booklet *Semachot*'s strident insistence that suicides are to receive no Jewish burial rites, we now have to also consider the Van Dusens and Margaret Battin who are united in their earnest hope that in the minds of more and more religious people, suicide "will become more usual and accept-able as the years pass."

THE RELIGIOUS AGENDA FOR THE FUTURE

The question of the religious response to the phenomenon of el-derly suicide will remain an emotionally charged and deeply per-plexing issue with which theologians, seminary professors of hu-man relations, denominational committees, clergy and lay leaders shall have to wrestle with in future years. I would only share one rabbi's conclusions and ask the reader's patience for a brief sidestep.

Centuries ago, the Talmudic sages constructed a means of pro-tecting the individual Jew from unintended ritual violations. This clever concept is known as *Siyag la-Torah*, "a fence around the law." You see, in effect, what the rabbis were doing was to arbitrarily extend and make more stringent the list of either proscribed foods or those activities which were permissible on the Sabbath and festivals. For instance, though beans and peas are not Biblically forbidden foods during the Passover season because of their kinship to grains, which are prohibited, these rabbis extended the prohibition to include such legumes. If one erects a fence of prohibition even wider than it necessarily must be, one would be most unlikely to ever actually violate the Biblically ordained precept.

Now, the unlikely connection is made from beans to suicide by considering just how easy it might be to enlarge upon that number of instances under which suicide might come to be viewed as an accepted and even sacramentalized alternative. Once, even under narrowly defined and carefully delineated circumstances, any given instance of suicide receives official sanction by a religious order or by a group, who is to say that those criteria might not become progressively widened and enlarged as additional exceptions are made for other individuals whose personal conditions are deemed to be desperate. No, with all due apologies to the Van Dusens and to the Concern for Dying group, such is not the path I would endorse. Religion will make a grave misstep were it to advocate or sacramentalize suicide. Faith is designed to be life-affirming and anything less is unthinkable.

Gerontologists have long expected the community of faith to play a profound role in the lives of older persons, a role that perhaps no other institution can fill as well. By the year 2000, some 32 million Americans will be 65 years of age and older, and within but a quarter of a century, the older population of this country will increase by more than one million people a year. A recent demographic study of the Jewish community of my city, Pittsburgh, Pennsylvania, only confirms this projection. The 1984 study proves that 21.6% of our community is now over the age of 65 — a percentage which has already doubled since 1976. [29]

For all of the reasons discussed earlier, potentially desperate and suicide-prone people will in future years be turning to both the synagogue and the church with desperate hopes for a spiritual antidote. We must be prepared with that special message of meaningfulness which perhaps only religion can impart.

During the solemn services for the Jewish High Holy Days, the liturgy reaches an emotional crescendo when the cantor intones the plaintive words of the psalmist: "Cast us not aside in time of old age. Forsake us not when our own strength is spent." There follows then the echoed response of the entire congregation as each worshipper, repeating the words of the cantor, becomes painfully aware of the fragility of life and of its vulnerability. "Cast us not aside . . . ." Gently, patiently, and convincingly, the religious community will have to be able to address the life situation of the elderly, to assuage their pain, their loneliness, and their diminished sense of self-worth. With William Cowper, the faith community must be able to credibly remind our elderly:

> Beware of desperate steps, the darkest day,
> Lived till tomorrow will have passed away.

If we are to meet this challenge in the future, ambitious models will need to be created *now* by experts commissioned by the separate denominations and their agencies, aimed at effectuating a workable response to the predicted arithmetic increase among the ranks of the elderly. Seminary curriculae will have to be reviewed and carefully redesigned to provide sorely needed emphasis on the psychological and spiritual needs of the elderly. Now such courses, more often than not, are offered as optional electives while much more money, energy and creativity are assigned to the ministries of youth, camping and special programs for college-age young people. The fact remains that today's seminarian is as unprepared to cope with the suicidal congregants as was I. They must read and discuss such useful articles as A. E. Bennett's clear analysis of the potential suicide[30] or Judith Haggerty's most readable and helpful profile of suicidal behavior among the elderly.[31] All of us, clergy and lay alike, need expert guidance in recognizing the suicide-prone elderly, and in becoming perceptive enough to read their cries for help.

Presbyteries, denominational and adjudicatory bodies will have to accept the role of coordinator for symposia on the spiritual well-being of the elderly. Issues which ought to be included for consideration might be:

— The proper programmatic role for both church and synagogue in ministering to the elderly.
— Opportunities for interfaith coalition building on behalf of the elderly.
— Theological and educational materials which ought to be com-

missioned as special devotional literature earmarked for the use of the elderly.

Future church-synagogue educational commissions will need to design curriculum offerings and commission necessary texts to broach any number of concerns and attitudes vis-à-vis aging and the elderly within Sunday School and adult education programs. Among such concerns would necessarily be:

— What does the Bible say about growing older?
— What can the old teach the young and vice versa?
— How does one speak with an aging parent?
— How does Judaism/Christianity allow us to deal inter-generationally?
— What makes life worth *continued* living?
— How can we find strength and hope when we feel like we've reached the end of the line?

Individual parishes and congregations, within the next decade or so, will see the need to establish "aging awareness committees." These will become as common as today's altar guild, youth group or sisterhood. What is more, the level of commitment to such programming will have to be far more ambitious than simply planning a few bus trips and covered dish suppers. Financial planning for retirement must be included within our ministry to the elderly. Clearly, foremost among the concerns of this age group is their understandable worry that longevity in years will outlive their personal financial resources. The temple and church must be willing to present program seminars in finance by professionals which will also offer specific financial counseling services. Alternatives to desperation must be offered to our elderly in a loving, competent and honest manner.

A new thrust toward inter-generational programming is urgently needed to validate our increasing awareness and understanding of the aging process. Temple Sinai in Pittsburgh, Pennsylvania, has discovered how Jewish genealogy may become an important instrument for cross-generational sharing. In this program, our sixteen-year-old confirmands have recently been sent out to the homes and apartments of some of our elderly temple members, who played a part in founding our congregation some 40 years ago, in order to record their memories and anecdotes. Not only will this data be-

come most valuable, as a Golden Anniversary volume is anticipated, but our elderly have become the living resources for the
young in helping to trace their own Jewish roots here in Pittsburgh.

For many of our teens, this project has offered their first occasion
to sit and talk at length with older temple members. Grandparents
frequently live far away, or have died, and our adolescents are receiving an eye-opening initiation disabusing them of many of the
stereotypes of the elderly. Our students have come back to our con-
firmation class and reported how really "neat" their designated in-
terviewee proved to be. There were frequent observations such as:
"You know, old people *can* be friendly," "They really knew a lot
about Temple Sinai that I had never known," "They were just like
me, only they were older," and "I was prepared for a real downer
but, you know what, I had a terrific time over there. I may go back
again, just for a visit."

Initially several of our elderly members, when approached to be
interviewed by our confirmants, responded with a shrug and "Why
me? What could I possibly know that would be of value to others?"
After these tapings, many of those interviewed have remarked as to
how much better they felt, and how many wonderful memories the
interviewing session brought back to them of our temple's formative
years. These individuals were reminded of their continued useful-
ness and of many of the accomplishments which they helped to
bring about. And if nothing else ever comes from those tapes, I for
one am well satisfied that they have served a positive good. Goethe
was so right when he noted the value of reflecting on the past: "He
is the happiest man who can see the connection between the end and
the beginning of his life."[32]

All signs point toward the validation of one of Nancy Osgood's
conclusions:

> In general, those who have a zest for life, who accentuate the
> positive, who feel they are in control of their own lives, who
> are fond of certain people, places or things, and who have a
> commitment to beliefs, values, or causes greater than them-
> selves are more likely to adapt successfully to the various
> stresses of late life.[33]

Surely the religious response should be to bolster such self-
awareness, and to help those who turn to us in their efforts to accen-
tuate the positive in their lives. Ministers, priests, rabbis and other

religious practitioners must be willing to listen empathically as the elderly pour out their feelings of guilt, of fear, of doubt. For many of them, such caregivers may be the only ones to whom they might turn. But we can sometimes do more than listen!

It may well be that providing short-term goals for the elderly which are realistic in nature may also serve to be of enormous assistance to those who are looking for some constructive framework around which to build the rest of their lives. For others, an important goal might be to help them understand, adjust and accept the aging process. Through open discussion, careful listening, and supportive prayer, many of the elderly may come to view aging in a more positive way, recognizing it as a period of possible change, growth and development.

CONCLUSION

Those religious practitioners who would endeavor to be of help to the suicide-prone elderly will need to bring to bear a keen awareness of the impact of multiple loss—health, beauty, spouse, friends, financial security—and the relationship between physical changes, pain, stress, and emotional problems. Moreover, equally crucial will be the ability to recognize and to accurately assess levels of depression and loneliness.

An inordinate challenge will await the church and synagogue vis-à-vis the growing ranks of the elderly. We must not be caught napping. All of the creativity, imagination and devotion which can be summoned will be needed to adequately respond in the future. "To be old is a wonderful thing," Martin Buber once wrote, "when one has not *unlearned* how to begin again." Buber's words are apt for our own times as the intellectual horizons widen and become limitless. Those who are 65 years of age may well live another 25 to 30 years, and who is to say that this final chapter of their lives should not be the very best. All that is required is an abiding faith in the *possibility* of a tomorrow. And keeping this fact in mind, the religious community must recognize the importance of suicide intervention among the elderly. Only then will we be able to join together in a new prayer for growing old:

> Blessed are You, O Lord our God, Sovereign of the universe who enriches the years of the aged with renewed hope and new understanding.

NOTES

1. Osgood, Nancy J. *Suicide in the Elderly* (Aspen Systems Corporation, Rockville, Maryland), p. 12.
2. *Ibid.*
3. Comfort, A. *Practice of Geriatric Psychiatry* (New York, Elsevier, 1980), pp. 79-81 as cited in "Suicide in the Elderly," by Bromberg, Shirley MD and Cassel, Christine K. MD, *Journal of the American Geriatric Society*, 1983, November 3, p. 699.
4. Resnik, H. C. "Suicide and Aging," *Journal of the American Geriatric Society*, 1970, 18:152.
5. Barraclough, B. M. "Suicide in the Elderly," *British Journal of Psychiatry* (Special publication 6), 1972, p. 87, cited in Bromberg, S. and Cassel, C., *Ibid.*
6. Osgood, Nancy J. *Ibid.*, p. 39.
7. *Ibid.*
8. *Ibid.*, p. 36.
9. *Ibid.*
10. Gardner, Bahn & Mach, 1964; Grollman, 1971; Kreitman, 1977; Resnik & Cantor, 1970; cited in Osgood, *Ibid.*, p. 12.
11. Batchelor & Napier, 1953; Benson & Brody, 1975; Dubin, 1963; McIntosh et al., 1981; O'Neale, Robins & Schmidt, 1965; cited in Osgood, *Ibid.*
12. Osgood, *Ibid.*, p. 13.
13. Osgood, *Ibid.*, pp. 26-27.
14. Seiden, R. 1983, November. "Suicide Among the Young and the Elderly," paper presented at the annual meeting of the Gerontological Society of America, San Francisco, cited in Osgood, *Ibid.*, p. 26.
15. Durkheim, E., *Suicide 1897-1951*, cited in Osgood, *Ibid.*, p. 39.
16. Rogow, I. 1973. "The Social Context of the Aging Self," *Gerontologist*, 12, pp. 82-87, cited in Osgood, *Ibid.*, p. 31.
17. *Semachot*, chapter 2 as cited by Freehof, S. In *American Reform Responsa*, Volume II (Central Conference of American Rabbis, New York, New York).
18. *Ibid.*
19. Benet, Rabbi Mordecai, 19th century in *Parashat Mordechai* "Yoreh De-ah" 25.
20. Eusebius, *Ecclesiastical History*, Book 8, Chapter 12, as cited by Phipps, Will E., "Christian Perspectives on Suicide," *The Christian Century*, October 30, 1985, p. 970.
21. *City of God*, Book I, Sections 18-26, *Ibid.*, p. 971.
22. Aquinas, *Summa Theologica* 2-2, q64,5, cited in Phipps, *Ibid.*
23. Dante, *Inferno*, Phipps, *Ibid.*
24. Bonhoeffer, *Ethics* (MacMillan Press, 1955), pp. 124-25, cited in Phipps, *Ibid.*
25. "Christian Perspectives on Suicide," *The Christian Century*, Phipps, William E., October 30, 1985, p. 971.
26. *Ibid.*
27. *Ibid.*, p. 972.
28. Van Dusen, Elizabeth, Suicide note, cited in *Ibid.*, p. 972.
29. *Pittsburgh Jewish Chronicle* (Pittsburgh, Pennsylvania), November 28, 1985, p. 1.
30. Bennett, A. E. *Geriatrics*, May, 1967, pp. 175-81.
31. Haggerty, Judith. "Suicide in the Aging," *Journal of Geriatrics and Psychiatry*, 1973, Vol. 7, pp. 43-69.
32. Butler, R. N. (1963). "Recall in Retrospection," *Journal of American Geriatric Society*, No. 11, p. 523.
33. Osgood, *Ibid.*, pp. 199-200.

Intergenerational Living and Worship: The Caring Community

Harold J. Hinrichs, DMin

SUMMARY. There are several conceptual and relational shifts required when "intergenerational," the dynamics of intentional community and liturgy, as the work of the people, are brought together. The Caring Community Project is a training resource to assist congregations in forming intentional, intergenerational communities. Shared power, authority, and responsibility expressed through the discipline of the steps of the liturgy, as described briefly in this paper, unfold a dynamic transforming process of change. Older persons are key advocates for this ministry and major beneficiaries of its care and development.

INTRODUCTION

Can the local church provide a functional surrogate, extended family community that will support, energize, and provide care for people of all ages, particularly frail elderly? This is one of the major questions facing the church as we approach the year 2000. This question challenges the basic assumptions about the function of the congregation and presses for the actualization of a new paradigm, as Fritjof Capra* and others are envisioning, for the major functional systems of our society. In our concern for older persons, is the reli-

Harold J. Hinrichs, Developer and Director of the Caring Community Project, is a family life and aging program specialist. He has served as a pastor, taught in seminaries, and developed a parish-based clinical pastoral education program. Dr. Hinrichs received his MDiv from Wartburg Theological Seminary, STM and DMin from Andover-Newton Theological School. For further information: Caring Community Project, 422 South Fifth Street, Minneapolis, Minnesota 55415.

*Fritjof Capra, author of *The Turning Point*, Bantam Books, 1982.

gious community consciously able to participate in such a transformation? The Caring Community Project experience suggests that there is a process which enables congregations to form intentional, intergenerational communities that appreciate the integration of life and worship. It began in a congregation in 1969 when a selected group of people met regularly for a year to ask: "How do people experience 'church' in the congregation? Is the experience of 'church' consistent with biblical and theological roots? Are the needs and experiences of people taken seriously?" The need for people to experience the church as community was obvious.

In 1970, a ministry training program for small groups began using the liturgy as a basic conceptual framework for the reflection process of the community experience, as part of the national staff of The American Small-Group Ministry training to prepare for the formation of intentional, intergenerational communities in congregations.

Twenty congregations began to use and explore the Caring Community Project over a three-year period. Since 1983, numerous congregations have been trained in the United States, West Germany, and Norway.

This creative approach to ministry provides congregations with steps to form intentional, intergenerational communities of 35 to 70 persons who gather for two hours each week for six to nine months. These communities are characterized by shared power, authority, and responsibility which emerges through the discipline of the liturgy. Liturgy is taken seriously as the work of the people. To begin this process, a clergy and a lay person are trained as a team. This team then shares the process with a core group of 12 to 15 people for 11 weeks. This core group, in turn, is the catalyst for the formation of a Caring Community within a parish. After this initial experience of six to nine months, the congregation will have the resources to plan the formation of numerous caring communities.

The Caring Community Project developed as a way to meet two distinctive but related needs. How does the church give people the experience of being in community — the body of Christ — rather than the experience of being fragmented and isolated? How does the church provide a system of support and care for persons in families and households that is no longer being provided by the biological family?

A NEW APPROACH

The process of change is always threatening, especially to institutions like the church, even though its basic proclamation is a promise of change and renewal. It is indeed difficult for most of us to take off our institutional hats, or pass its assumptions, in order to be creatively reflective about the life of the church. It is very easy to become negative and vocal like a fearful youth who blames parents for all that is not going well. However, we must accept the responsibility as believing persons to share our critical observation and reflection about life in the congregation. We are not talking about something hypothetical but rather that relational community promised by the gospel for which we yearn; many, however, have cynically given up on that promise as an idyllic illusion of the past.

Leaders base sermons and Bible studies on Paul's powerful image of the church as the body of Christ: "Where one hurts, the whole body hurts; where one rejoices, the whole body rejoices together." What would it be like if that really happened? Some quickly defend the status quo by giving isolated examples of individuals who care for others. In the time of crisis, a person or family may be surrounded by an obvious display of affection and support. However, while the image of community is deeply rooted in the biblical tradition, it is hardly a functional expectation in present congregational life.

Most people experience the church on Sunday mornings as spectators to a traditionally prescribed worship form. There may be an educational opportunity for the young and the more active adults, but there is generally very little conscious awareness of any need for intergenerational activity that enables people to experience "koinonia" wherein needs are shared, spiritual bonding occurs, people are energized, and "diakonia" is empowered. The norm is fragmentation in congregational life. Worship is unrelated to education, and neither are responsive to what is happening in the lives of the people. Clergy are assumed to be in charge, in control, and thereby are expected to know what is best for everyone, particularly about spiritual matters. "Spiritual" is functionally defined in a very narrow way that focuses on another world, namely, past biblical times and heaven in the future. There is usually some kind of hierarchical "pecking order" within the congregational politics with the often clear understanding that people will not get too personal or too close in their relationships. This may be overstated, but these primary dynamics are definitely present in most congregations. What we face is a need for a major shift or transformation; more is needed than just a "beefing-up" of any one component such as a more lively worship, a change of pastorate, or an increase in shut-in visits.

Older persons are vital keys to this transformation process because they have the memory and wisdom of the past. A few years ago I asked my mother to tell me about the changes that have taken place in the church in her lifetime. "That's easy," she exclaimed. "First, I remember when men sat on one side of the church and women sat on the other. Let me see. Then, I would say (a change happened) when we switched from German to English (that betrays my heritage)." After a brief pause she said, "I'm on my fourth or fifth hymnal." We then began to talk about the significance of those changes and how those changes were stimulated. Older persons know about change.

How did these changes come about? My mother and I concluded, after long speculation, that children were probably the catalysts for the changes. "Mommy, Daddy, why do I have to sit here in church? Why can't I sit over there?" "Why do we have to go to church and speak German when we speak English everywhere else?" "Why do we need to sing and pray 'thees' and 'thous' in church; we don't talk like that!"

Children obviously didn't make the decisions to make the changes. Nevertheless, they influenced older people who somehow indicated that it was okay to change. I asked my mother if she wanted to go back to any of the previous situations. She said, "Of course not!" Older persons have memories and stories, and while change does not come easy in the church, it does happen. It needs to happen.

Older people are essential, not only because of their perspective on history, but because they may also be the catalysts for change in the future. Their contribution to the content of the life of the community — its need to be intergenerational — is particularly important. Without authentic intergenerational involvement, there is little possibility to integrate faith and life. Older persons, however, need to experience a genuine desire to be included in community, to know their contribution is respected and valued, and that they will be cared about with dignity as persons.

Who remembers growing up in the extended family? The family or clan would bring itself together regularly around events often connected to the life of faith — baptisms, weddings, funerals, anniversaries, as well as birthdays, holidays, and special occasions like graduation. This informal support system was the source of stories, traditions, and information shared across the generations.

Families no longer gather as they once did. Because of mobility, most biological extended families are scattered around the country. Yet the need for supportive communities is unending. Do families realize their importance as a functional intergenerational support system? Do families see their function as a supportive community related in a significant way to understanding and experiencing the life of faith? Is there a relationship between the need for people to experience "church" as a supportive community—the body of Christ—and the loss of the extended family as a viable support system? The congregation provided a worship service, a supplemental educational program, and the services of a pastor. The church, particularly the local congregation, has continued to provide a Sunday worship service, a supplemental educational program grouped by age levels, and the pastoral services of clergy. Have congregational leaders discussed the need for intergenerational supportive communities? It doesn't happen automatically, even if we lead Sunday morning worship to the best of our abilities. The need for the congregation to provide leadership in the formation of intentional, intergenerational communities for people is very new for all of us.

THE CARING COMMUNITY

When an intergenerational community of 35 to 70 persons is formed, people gather early on a weekday evening. Fifty to 70 persons may be the maximum size of the family or clan (perhaps larger than the communities of the New Testament churches). These same people gather each week for two hours for six to nine months. There needs to be the intentionality of each person to attend and to share in the responsibility of the community. There are no spectators. There needs to be enough time to be together over an extended period (with an ending time) to avoid the development of tightly closed groups.

LITURGY

Liturgy literally means the work of the people. However, most people associate liturgy with a prescribed order of worship that directs the internal behavior of the congregation within the sanctuary, from the words to say, to when to stand or sit. A clergyperson is clearly in charge, regardless of the centrality of the pulpit or the altar in the worship setting. This worship context has historically been referred to as the sanctuary or holy place where people meet God's presence. By association, people assume they are to leave the secular world or human concerns "outside" and come into the presence of the sacred within the building. In this framework, liturgy is experienced as a formula of biblical or "spiritual" words with no intent of sharing personal, familial, or "secular" concerns.

Recapturing liturgy as the work of the people is a key element in reorienting congregational life to provide the milieu in which people may share and reflect on their life from the reference of powerful faith symbols. Does invocation have only to do with beginning a worship service or does invocation have to do with calling each person to life-long ministry? Do confession, absolution, and forgiveness have to do only with those "serious" sins? Do we disclose the truth of how we feel about ourselves, our bodies, our aging, our pain, our fear of dying to God in isolation? Do we disclose the truth in the presence of God to a brother or sister in Christ? Liturgy, with this content, encompasses life itself and sharing this content in the community of faith transforms isolated individuals into bonded fellowships. There, worship, learning, "koinonia," "diakonia," and witness are integral aspects of the whole.

To begin intentional caring communities, three conceptual shifts need to be made. These shifts have their basis in a relational understanding of theology of community that is dynamically called forth from our baptism into Christ, and from our being joined together into the community of faith, the body of Christ. *First*, rather than picturing the presence or power of God as primarily external on the altar or up in heaven, the presence or power of God in Christ needs to be envisaged as internally present or within each person equally in the community. *Second*, rather than perpetuating a hierarchical authority structure, clergy need to literally move beside people so that everyone is equally necessary for the whole community's function. *Third*, it is through shared power and authority that "response-ability" can be shared, not just for what happens when together "in the sanctuary," but also for that which happens for life in the world. The impact and power of these shifts emerges through the experience of the liturgy. As the liturgy is absorbed as a faith reflection framework, the action of ministry begins in the world.

INVOCATION

The two-hour liturgy begins with invocation. The basis of invocation links us to our entrance into the community through baptism. It is a constant reminder of the action of God's creation, of Christ's redemptive kingdom, and of the Spirit's empowerment. Rather than being a time to call upon God through worship, the invocation is a time of being called together by God in community. Each person has been living each moment of life "in-vocation," in God's calling. Rather than the invocation as the signal to sit still for the next hour, it is a time to reflect on the depth, newness, and power of being and having been "in-vocation" to God in very personal and specific ways.

"In the name of God . . . Amen!" The ancient baptismal formula signals the time for the community to reflect on their calling card. Who are we? Whose are we? We are each named by God and called by God to be the persons we were created to become. Called to be your self, physically, emotionally, intellectually, spiritually, to live out your God-given identity. That calling begins in faith, is formalized in baptism, and continues into our death. Each person takes "response-ability" for themselves. We cannot respond for others.

We are "in-vocation," in God's calling to be ourselves to those persons in our households, to our calling as we are students, workers, or in our third age, citizens, and to our calling to care for the earth or environment. During this brief reflection time, the persons in the community reflect on being named by God, being assured of Christ's presence during the past week in all situations, and being called and sent by God to live a ministry of reconciliation or restoration in the world. As people in the community know each other by name and grow to depend on each other for support, people begin to sense the importance of their ministry in the world.

CONFESSION/ABSOLUTION/FORGIVENESS

The second step in the liturgy process is the time for confession, absolution, and forgiveness. The community divides into small "family" groups of six or seven persons. These family groups are intergenerational, have the same members each week, and generally do not have people from the same household. Confession is making oneself known to God and to each other. At the same time, absolution is the experience of being confronted with acceptance, being heard, listened to by God in Christ through the community. Forgiveness is the response, "the Amen!" to the pronouncement of renewal, wholeness, redemption, forgiveness, relationship in Christ.

Each person is individually given opportunity to confess, make known in the family group, "How was it living with yourself this week?" "How was it in your household?" "How was it at school, at work, in retirement?" "How was your citizenship?" "How was your care of the earth?" This is not a therapy time, story time, or probe time. The persons in the family group have the task of hearing and accepting. This is a very powerful and healing time for many people. These 15 to 20 minutes go quickly.

WORD

During the next 45-minute time period, the whole community gathers to work with the Word for the week. The texts are usually the same as those used in the parish that week taken from the lectionary. The task is for the community to encounter what is the new action that God is calling forth through people in the world.

The texts are read and the historical circumstances are explored. This may be through simple drama, story telling, or other appropriate information to engage the community in action. From the historical encounter, the emphasis switches to the existential questions: What is God calling forth, acting now? Again role plays or various art forms may be used to open people to the action of God in their lives through the Word. This approach forces people to take responsibility for what is happening in their experience. Each person's experience varies, and if these perspectives are shared, everyone is enriched. Here, the experiences of the elderly are invaluable as resources to gain insight into understanding God's action in the human situation.

CREED

After the community struggles with the Word for the day, it is time for each person to confront the question, "What are you going to do about that Word this week?" Now the community divides into

the family groups they were in during confession, absolution, and forgiveness for 10 to 15 minutes. After a brief meditation period, each person declares a particular stance as their primary ministry for the week. It is their response to the Word that is being called forth from them. Does the Word focus a stance about self? Is the stance of ministry focused in the household, at school, at work, in retirement? Is the stance related to citizenship or care for environment? There is an obvious link to "in-vocation." This Creed time or stance-taking enables the participants to image and focus on specific action as ministry. As people share their stances, they take responsibility and are accountable to live out their action. Creed becomes a very dynamic stance-taking time which involves creation, the kingdom of God, and the empowerment of an incarnating Spirit.

OFFERING

Next, the whole community gathers to present and offer their stances of ministry as their offerings to God to be lived in service to the world. Specific actions of ministry and concerns are shared in prayer. Bread and wine are tangible symbols of the gifts. As these symbols of transformation are placed before the community and received, so individual gifts—stances of ministry—are received to be transformed into service. "Create in me a clean heart, O God, and renew a right spirit within me." People begin to discover that in Christ, all of life is transformed. Everything becomes ministry.

COMMUNION

Finally, the community celebrates the Body of Christ. Bread and wine are blessed, taken, broken or poured, and shared. This broken, restored people may now "discern the Body." In Christ they are joined to God and in Christ joined to each other. They are the Body. "Take and eat; this is my body," they say, as they look each other in the eye. "Take, drink, all of you; this is my blood; do this to remember me." People embrace as they share the prayer of peace, "Shalom," with each other. The community celebrates the Body of Christ.

BLESSING – GOING FORTH

The familiar blessing from the ages sends people back into the world to do their work, to do their service. This disciplined, rhythmic flow goes on as people scatter and gather again in the same process, but with ever new content as they experience life, reflect on it, and act again. The inner wholeness of individuality expands. While grounded and connected internally in Christ, life is focused for renewal in the external world in the name of the same Christ.

I was visiting a Caring Community in a congregation that had been meeting for about two months and enjoying a simple soup supper before the evening liturgy began. I was sitting at a round table between two little girls, about nine or ten years old. We were conversing about school, the town, the Caring Community, and their interests when I asked, "What do you want to be when you grow up?" Immediately, one little girl said, "I want to be like her and her." She was pointing at the two oldest people in the community who were sitting across the table from us. Then I asked, "Well, how come?" "Because they both like kids!" came the quick reply. These people were not biologically related, but in a matter of months, a bonding, a knowing had been realized. How better would you teach children positive attitudes about aging and the elderly?

Congregations or adults in general have a definite bias about having children present as viable contributors to the life of Christian community. Only when communities struggle to discover children as persons do they begin to take everyone seriously as individuals. This is true for elderly as well as younger adults. This struggle points to the need for openness to new ideas and to the necessity of learning through experience, reflection, and action.

IMPLICATIONS

Integrating life and faith in the liturgy within intergenerational communities addresses numerous issues for the church in ministry with older persons. Several examples have already been mentioned; however, some further illustrations may be helpful to visualize further the potential impact of the Caring Community.

Health care is clearly a major issue facing our society. One of the basic needs is that people take responsibility for the care of themselves. The vocation to health as a call from God emerging from our baptism is an essential connection. How we eat, exercise, think, and feel about ourselves has roots in our spirituality. Older persons also may be challenged in their vocation as citizens locally and globally to influence public policy to undergird the health care of people.

Voluntary care for the elderly is another important concern. Is it possible for people who are not biologically related to become bonded in community to the point where volunteer hands-on care becomes a natural result? I know of a college student who was away from family while in school who participated in a Caring Community. One night, the biblical text triggered in him the fact that he had not known or been close to his grandfather. That night he asked the pastor if he could visit an elderly person. He was referred to "Ed," who was in a nursing home. The following week, the young man brought Ed to the Caring Community. Over the next few weeks, Ed influenced that community in many ways by who he was, as well as what he called forth from the community.

Shared housing is another example that emerged in another Caring Community. A young, single teacher moved to town. She lived alone and joined a congregation with a Caring Community. An older couple in the same Caring Community happened to have space in their home. Within two months, these people bonded and formed one household. How could congregations begin to "broker" the available housing in a way that would be natural and helpful?

Respite care and support for caregivers are possibilities built-in to the potential resources of a congregation with Caring Communities. Another obvious example is linking children with older persons or older persons with single-parent households. There are many individual illustrations of the potential of the Caring Community.

Two major barriers exist for the Caring Community. One is the impact of theological training. Clergy are generally trained and taught to think in fragmented specialization. The traditional and hierarchical approach to parish life is generally uncritically assumed and perpetuated. Liturgy is unrelated to pastoral care and education. Rarely are the "practical disciplines" integrated with biblical studies and theological reflection. Clergy have little experience working alongside of people to develop leadership skills that empower rather than control. Theological training needs to be put back into the context of people who are living ministry, thinking theologically about everyday life. To prepare clergy to assist in that process is hardly the notion learned at seminaries.

The second barrier to the Caring Community is institutional preoccupation. When the external pattern of congregational life is established, it is very difficult to change. Since Constantine, the authority of the church has been focused in the clergy. Sunday morning is primarily a fixed and prescribed process. We construct buildings that speak a message theologically, often counter to our purpose. We experience power struggles and isolation.

The hope is with people — particularly older people — who are not fully disillusioned but still looking for hope. The church is people. The liturgy is the work of people. No one can do liturgy for someone else or be the church for someone else. The exciting possibilities that are kindled by people in church who are doing Caring Community press for the continual promise of transformation. Intergenerational living and worship *is* a reality with the promise of transforming possibilities.

Communities Within Communities

O. Z. White, MDiv, PhD

SUMMARY. "Communities within communities" is a description of certain programs existing in San Antonio, Texas, which involve a number of the elderly who reside in the area. The theoretical base for the discussion was that of Ferdinand Toennies' Gemeinshaft/Gesellschaft, and the description involved the satisfactions derived by the elderly from participating in programs which demonstrate some of those attributes described as "Gemeinschaft-like" in opposition to the Gesellschaft-like world.

Sociologists have through the years attempted to denote and describe a qualitative difference in the way that people relate to each other in their shared life spaces. Ferdinand Tonnies sought to delineate between two model intellects, the natural will (Wesenville) and the rational will (Kurville). While neither is operative to the exclusion of the other, Tonnies described those social relationships in which the natural will predominates (Wesenville) as Gemeinschaft. The rational will (Kurville) is what is prevalent in Gesellschaft societies.[1]

The prototype for Gemeinschaft relationships is the family, where there is face-to-face interaction, the bonds are durable, individual members are irreplacable (there are substitutes, but it's not the same), and each member is valued for his or her own sake. Resting on sentiment and understanding (community, though Tonnies himself did not to my knowledge use that specific term in the sense of territorial communities) these relationships evidence intimacy, full-

O. Z. White is Professor of Sociology, Trinity University, San Antonio, Texas. He earned the AB and MA degrees at Furman University, the MDiv degree at Erskine Theological Seminary, and the PhD from Emory University.

ness, informality, trust, and are operative in a world of integrated institutions in which change is slow and deliberate. The Gemeinschaft person says, "I am my brother's keeper," and basks in the joy of seeing good jobs well done; his/her central question is, "what is the need?"

The prototype for Gesellschaft persons is the city, where interaction is manipulative and is based on bonds which are transient, goal-oriented and impersonal. There is a transient quality to it all; the individual members are role players and there is a means-ends oriented value structure. These relationships are characterized by distance, rationality, fragmentation, formality, and legality. They live in a world of disintegrated institutions which are competitive and even hostile and coercive. The Gesellschaft person says, "nobody owns me," and demands to know, "what's my pay?" and "what can I get out of this?"

Ideal types such as Gemeinschaft/Gesellschaft are, of course, heuristic fictions — they have no counterpart in reality to the extent that they would appear in the real world in any pure sense. (If so, they would indeed be rare.) Their functions are to serve as extreme examples — standards of behavior by means of which a specific group or population can be described. There have been numerous attempts to fit polar typologies into quantifiable research; some have met with success, and others have not. Whether really real or not, Tonnies articulated in a systematic way concepts which have been floating around since Aristotle: the size and density of a population effects the personalities, life styles, and value systems of those who reside within its boundaries.

Social scientists have often described networks of relationships in the context of community theory. The typical Gemeinschaft-life community was relatively small, it was a specified physical space with identifiable boundaries, and there were resources within that space by means of which all the social and physical needs of the membership were met. Without belaboring the obvious, let it be said that the influence of the city and the fact of a population characterized by mobility has led to a number of efforts to reinterpret community in the light of perceived population shifts and social change. For those who are classified as "older Americans" there continues to be a tendency to see traditional communities with the Gemeinschaft-life characteristics as the "good old days." (And indeed, this has been one of the major criticisms of Tonnies' work.)

People long for the security, the moral and ethical certainties which accompany traditional relationships and integrated institutions, the sense of permanence in the absence of any rapid and unanticipated change. Gemeinschaft oriented people live in small worlds which are socially, physically, and psychologically secure. Gesellschaft people live in worlds in which the only constant is change, and the changing social climates cause a disconcerting relativity most evident in the fragmentation of institutions — at times a dissonance concerning the apparent weakness of morals and ethics.

Communities are ersatz: ("We are pleased to announce the opening of a wonderful new residential community, with new homes available at a cost of less than $200,000.00!") Changes appear to be accelerating at an exponential rate, and there appears to most that there is little if any predictive reliability related to most of their lives. Little matter that most of the elderly have had little if any personal experience with the kind of community they now long for: they think it was real, and for them, at least, that's all that counts.

There have been a number of attempts to recapture (or capture) those perceived functional elements of the past in a systematic way in order to either (1) identify where those elements presently exist, or (2) create social environments which would be conducive to the development of desired traits. It is not the purpose of this essay to deal with any of them on a theoretical level. Rather, we will attempt to delineate some of those social and psychological needs which many older people manifest and articulate, and report multiservice programs in San Antonio, Texas, which are in the early stages of meeting some needs for those who reside within their immediate residential area.

Today, communities do not exhibit institutional completeness; "community" simply means the immediate social context of the individual's life, if community is conceived of in terms of space and daily routines. Certainly, in the light of the mobility of most Americans, community is seldom an appropriate description of a neighborhood. The place of residence for many is not all that significant for the performance of daily routines. The term community has also been applied to universities; college and university administrators like to speak of the "academic community," as though a spectrum of basic loyalties and identifications resided there. At best, the academic "community" is a subculture and should be discussed using the vocabulary of subcultural analysis; more likely, it is a bureaucratic workplace where numbers of individuals market their professional skills. The term has also been applied to prisons, convents, mental hospitals, homes for the aged, and the like. Erving Goffman suggested that these can be best understood and described as "total institutions."[2]

It has occasionally been found to be physically helpful and emotionally rewarding when Gemeinschaft-like elements are nurtured in some form of community-like context in order to deliver services to older people. Church-oriented services can sometimes be successful when packaged in this way. The Church has seen itself as being a fellowship of believers, held together, bonded together by a common confession and a particular (some would say peculiar) kind of loving concern for one another, to the exclusion of at least some unbelievers. This loving concern should (and often does) radiate out to those who are neighbors in need.

Older people do, in fact, have certain concerns which are motivated by and express Gemeinschaft-like feelings. Bureaucratic structures have tended to develop in response to the needs of older people. This has been a matter of necessity in a rational world which reacts to needs which become apparent within a segment of a large and varied population. The bottom line of the bureaucracy is efficiency, which is a necessary attribute in the delivery of goods and services to large numbers of people. There must be rules, there must be order, there must be rational decision makers who often have physical and social distance from the clientele they serve. A bureaucracy can be seen as an organized set of skills for the most efficient production of a product or service.

All institutions have felt the impact of bureaucratic styles and approaches. Families have at the same time been enriched and victimized. The church is today a bureaucracy if it is anything at all. The problem is that as such bureaucracies do not have hearts or feelings. And as such they are not equipped to render the kinds of emotional feedback and support which the elderly, through their earlier socialization, have been programmed to expect. Those certainties and strengths of the past have been replaced; today, needs are met by rational and impersonal structures. Often, those needs are discussed in secrecy (a typical bureaucratic trait) by faceless people seated around long, skinny tables.

Goode wrote of "communities within communities."[3] What he was referring to was what he saw as being sometimes present in the professions in response to certain inner needs and outside pressures. What is being suggested here is that other types of communities within communities are possible — segments of the population of a given organization who become bonded together in some kind of relationship to the elderly. The communities we are describing are service communities, i.e., helping groups which have significant numbers of elderly people active as servers.

People are time-binding creatures; past and future are as important to one's sense of identity as the present. Destroy the past with all its ideal models, and there is a crisis in identity. With the elderly, the future is always in question, bringing about varying degrees of a crisis in hope. The professional insensitivity (understandable, but no less disconcerting) of those who help the elderly makes it seem that the promises of the past are empty. It is not difficult to understand their estrangement. For the church, it is not that they always find themselves outsiders in a physical sense. In the most pathetic manifestations of these problems, we find the elderly *in* but not *of* the group. "Clubs" for older church members abound: the "ABC," the "Keen Agers," the "Golden Agers," etc. There is an age-based segregation often in evidence which adds an obvious powerlessness to the estrangement which is already present.

Some examples of communities are operating in San Antonio, Texas. The purpose here is not to present a "how to" model; there are obviously a number of social and physical environmental factors which have led to the success of these programs, not the least of these being the leadership available and the high percentage of elderly who reside in the area. Southwest Texas is particularly attractive to large numbers of retired military because of a good housing market, the availability of military hospitals, and the mild climate. It is believed, however, that in modified forms these programs will work in almost any area in the United States.

THE CHRISTIAN ASSISTANCE MINISTRY

The Christian Assistance Ministry arose in response to problems faced by ministers of the downtown churches of San Antonio. "Street people" and individuals and families who had emergency needs appeared daily in churches asking for help. Most pastors have no formal training in social work and often could not fully comprehend the nature and extent of the expressed needs. Often they were unaware of help that would be available. Often the pastors themselves were unavailable, and uneasy (and sometimes understandably frightened) secretaries and staff persons were the only ones to cope. Some of the larger and more wealthy churches were beginning to install elaborate security procedures.

What usually happened was that some were given doles from discretionary funds, or sent away without guidance or counsel. As would be expected, there were many instances of people going from church to church with the same story, getting handouts or refusals from each. When an intoxicated street person who had not received aid was found dead under the shrubbery of First Presbyterian Church, the dynamic young pastor (Louis Zbinden) became the organizer and moving force behind the development of "CAM." (This is impressionistic at best, but it is suspected that most service communities begin out of the interaction between felt needs and dynamic personalities.)

A group of downtown churches agreed to pay regular dues to the new organization, and the congregations donated food and clothing. A director who was a social worker was employed, and in time two additional part-time social workers were added to the staff. While records on the age of clients have not been kept, there is agreement that a significant number of them are over the age of 60. Counselors are all trained volunteers who work four-hour shifts once a week. While retirement is not a requirement, those most available for volunteering are those without a regular commitment to a work schedule.

Aid to families is on the basis of immediate need, and those who qualify for welfare from some existing agency are referred, along with careful followup. Many are people who have "fallen between the cracks." Their money has been stolen; they have lost their food stamps; relatives have been visiting from Mexico, and they used their food stamps up; they have immediate needs related to family disintegration, etc. The transients have often heard of the great climate and a surplus of jobs in the sun belt, or their cars have broken down and they have no money for continuing, or they were beaten and robbed, or they have become sick. Many are simply transients — a way of life they have chosen — and they want a free lunch and perhaps a warm coat or some clean clothes.

Thirty churches now contribute resources and volunteers; those churches in the suburban areas have responded to the needs far more than was expected. The program receives no funding other than that revenue generated from the churches plus some donations from individuals. As would be expected, CAM volunteers have a strong sense of identification with their work and with each other. It is hypothesized that this is based on several factors. It is a community of understanding in that those who are involved with this level of poverty realize that the stereotypes applied to those who are in need don't really apply to individuals. Also, it is a goal-oriented process, and those involved realize the importance of their work ("those children wouldn't eat tonight if it hadn't been for us!") and they enjoy and appreciate the success which has been evident there. CAM now sees well over 100 clients a day. Also, when many volunteers have reached the age where friends are rather hard to come by, warm, loving, personal relationships abound.

SAN ANTONIO METROPOLITAN MINISTRIES

This program grew out of CAM, in that housing needs became obvious through the CAM experience. There has been a major shortage of beds available to those who need shelter. As is common in many urban areas, many people were sleeping in doorways, under bridges, in public parks and vacant lots, and in abandoned houses. The existing shelters (Salvation Army, the Rescue Missions) had, and continue to have, rules which allow only a few nights' shelter (usually three) without charge. At the beginning of the program, the First Presbyterian Church used its gymnasium for a make-shift shelter. This year, the City of San Antonio has provided an old hotel which was in an area targeted for a major renewal effort. Under great pressure from the membership of the churches (generally a very conservative group in San Antonio), the city also provided funding for the renovation of the structure so that it would be usable. As with CAM, a number of the volunteers are retirees.

Services are provided non-judgmentally: those who come to SAMM seeking shelter for the night are not refused, no matter how many times they have been there before, so long as they obey the few simple rules necessary for health and safety. Sandwiches and a beverage are served in the evening, and again in the morning before it is necessary to leave; nobody (except on rare occasions) is allowed to stay in the shelter during the daylight hours. Chapel services are available each night, but are not mandatory. A private foundation has provided the funds for a medical clinic. The director is an early retiree who serves in that capacity for $1.00 a year; other staff persons are former street people who have "found a home" there.

Entire families are cared for as families, and a limited number of apartment-like spaces are available so that they are not forced to stay in the open dormitory. A minimum of eight volunteers are counselors each night, rotating among the churches. They also prepare and serve the food. The volunteers spend the night, acting as general helpers and as watchpeople. Staff members are always present in case of fights, etc. (this type of problem seldom arises).

As with CAM, there is in evidence strong ties among caregivers. Current records are not being kept with regards to the age of the clients, but a conservative estimate would be that a minimum of 25% of the SAMM residents are over 50. At the present time they get no special treatment, and none is anticipated. The goals are not (and never have been) in any sense long-term care. One purpose is to channel clients, if they so desire, into those agencies which have specific expertise and resources available and match the needs of the clients. While the volunteer groups are more transient in SAMM, there is at the same time a sense of identity, emotional ties, and a sense of purpose and caring. There is again the bond of special knowledge related to the fact that the stereotypes are misleading. Again, the volunteers are not all elderly; nobody asks about age. The fact that not all are old has been one of the reasons the experience has been rewarding to so many. (This can be assumed in view of the success of the two programs, the low turnover among volunteers, and the increasing number of churches that have become involved.) Here again there is an area in the lives of the older volunteers where they are not isolated; they are part of an important enterprise, and the nature and extent of their involvement is not determined on the basis of age; if they are physically able to do it and they want to do it, they do it.

JEFFERSON AREA COMMUNITY OUTREACH FOR OLDER PEOPLE, INC.

While the programs described above are in the inner city and reach out to the homeless and other poor who have emergency needs, the "Jefferson Co-Op" is a suburban program specifically designed to help the frail elderly so that the necessity of nursing home or hospital care can be postponed as long as possible. The clients of the Co-Op are middle class. The Jefferson area is a suburb of San Antonio which came into existence immediately before and after the Second World War.

The young adults who moved into this area have now become a part of the older generation, and many of them still reside there. It is not that they lack resources; the neighborhood is largely made up of small, neatly-kept houses which line quiet streets. Most of the older residents are retired military or retired civil servants. The clients to this point are ambulatory; it is recognized that soon they won't be. Others — some not quite as old, and some as old but not as frail — have organized a helping community in response to the needs of those around them. The entire community is a conservative one, and yet this group has been able to reach out across the traditional social and religious boundaries to participate in an enterprise which is so vitally important to them all. A list of the groups which participate underscores the degree of interaction which has taken place:

> Agudas Achim Synagogue (conservative)
> Grace Presbyterian Church
> Jefferson Methodist Church
> Los Angeles Heights Methodist Church
> Manor Baptist Church
> Morningside Manor Retirement Community
> St. Mary Magdalen Catholic Church
> Trinity Episcopal Church
> University Park Baptist Church
> Woodlawn Christian Church
> Zion Lutheran Church

It is rare indeed in Texas to have Roman Catholics, Baptists, and Jews joining together with other groups to form an honest interfaith effort in order to serve neighbors.

The original goal of the organization was to make sure that neighbors who are elderly get at least one good, nutritious meal a day. The first offering was a meal in one of the institutional buildings. Recognizing that many of the elderly in the community were unable to get themselves presentable and get to the place where the meal was being served, a "mobile meals" program was added. Meals are prepared in the kitchen of Morningside Manor Retirement Community and delivered by volunteers to the homes, at a minimal cost to the recipients. (The interest and support and the provision of expert consultation by Morningside Manor have been very valuable to the program in general.)

A second need which has been addressed by the Co-Op has been that of transportation. Groceries and household needs must be purchased; there are necessary visits to physicians, dentists, clinics, etc. There are needs for trips to the barber and beauty shop. The volunteers respond to most requests, using personal cars. As might be expected, there are some bizarre requests, but as much as possible the volunteers try to meet the felt needs. This type of mobility contributes greatly to the quality of life of the clients, and even though they are no longer able to travel at will, at least they can continue to participate in the day-by-day rituals, such as choosing and purchasing their own soap and making choices as to which cereals they will purchase.

"Handi-Neighbor" is an effort on the part of the Co-Op to meet simple repair needs which occur in households. There are limits to what they will do (one couple requested that their kitchen be rebuilt, and were nonplussed when they were refused), and problems related to liability have never been fully resolved; but this program continues to be active and relatively problem-free. Lamps are fixed, loose flooring is repaired, screens are installed, and perhaps most importantly, numerous ramps have been installed for those who have become wheelchair bound.

Telephone Reassurance is a program designed to have volunteers visit by telephone with lonely shut-ins. A minimal amount of necessary information is collected so there can be a quick response to any type of emergency and there can be quick follow-up when those called do not respond. The director of the reassurance network is herself a shut-in. The volunteers in this case are college students. It has been found that this pairing up of the young with the old has led to the development of many warm and meaningful relationships. But also, it has been a significant learning experience for the young people who have participated. Since young people seem to be very mobile, the director keeps careful track of all those involved so that substitutes are always readily available to either replace or substitute.

There is also a catch-all category called "Outreach." Assistance is available on an individual basis to those persons who need help in dealing with any of the other problems which might arise when elderly people continue to live independently.

The organizational structure of the Co-Op is as loose and unstructured as possible. At one point a large grant was given, a professional person was employed as director, and there was an attempt to extend services. What was encountered more than anything else was an increasing bureaucratization and constant efforts to recruit and train additional staff. The religious groups made a conscious decision to forego the outside funding in favor of having an organization directed by a director, herself a retiree, who is paid only a minimal amount supplementing her social security benefits. Organizations will agree to accept primary responsibility for a specific project for a specific period of time. This never excludes the participation of the members of other congregations. There is never an excess of funds, there are never too many volunteers and, as would be expected, there is always some friction. As a community within a community, it has brought to those who participate, both as givers and receivers, those rewards we learned to expect only in days gone by.

THE NEW GEMEINSCHAFT

Projections are always dangerous; social scientists (above all, perhaps) have terrible records when it comes to these kinds of predictive exercises. At the same time, the prediction of behavior is one of the basic reasons for the existence of these disciplines. In awareness of our bad track records, and recognizing the partial and tentative nature of the data upon which these predictions are made, we put forward the following suggestions.

One prediction which is safe barring some major catastrophe has to do with sheer numbers; the elderly as a specific category will continue to be more and more significant in our population. People are living longer, and there will probably be a continuing increase until the "war babies" (the oldest now being 40 years old) all reach the elderly category. This means that there will be a growing number of institutions which are dedicated to this particular cohort. Since an increasing number of these people will be healthy, more than ever they will be politically active and they will grow even stronger as a special interst group. Since the liberal politicians are the ones who most often respond to social needs of disenfranchised groups, the elderly will be more and more responsive to liberal politicians and liberal causes in order to maintain their own security as related to such things as Medicare, Medicaid, and other Social Security benefits.

If the above prediction is true, and the results follow, we will have a population which consists of a more financially-independent elderly than we have ever known before. This will have a profound effect on the churches. As in all institutions of our society, numbers and money mean power. The church will then move from being a church *for* the old to being a church *of* the old. (As an unreconstructed cynic I would predict that this will be interpreted as an insight from Liberation Theology even though it will be difficult indeed to equate the poor of the third world to the old of the United States.) At any rate, they will be more difficult to compartmentalize, less satisfied with pious platitudes, and more critical of general church programs and plans. This will mean, among other things, that *gemeinschaft* will be reborn in the life of the church as healthy, mobile, active elderly meet in ritualized situations in awareness of the fact that they are far from being mere recipients of the church's largesse. In other words, the "communities within communities" will not be simply helped and helpers but also expediters and planners who are active participants in every phase of the community process.

One of the problems of Christianity in the 20th century has been that while most people in the United States believe it and identify with it, few people have seen themselves as having time to practice it very often. The new communities will have plenty of time. The problem will be that of relating in a meaningful way the traditional theology of the church to a suddenly dynamic and questing group. This could have a radical effect on every level of education within the church if the potentials are exploited.

The communities to which future elderly will relate will, it is predicted, be more capable of meeting the needs of the elderly individuals who belong. Those who are reaching retirement age are already able to relate better; they have not anticipated an old age surrounded by loving grandchildren and doting children; rather, they have lived in a world where *their* children left the nest not long before their own parents retired. They will not expect as much, nor will they be as unprepared for this new status in the life cycle. Communities within communities will be a welcome relief to them: it will entail far more freedom and creativity than they are presently led to expect.

Hopefully, this will have a domino effect not only in the Church, but in communities at large as well. The poor and the homeless, for example, will have as their advocates large numbers of relatively independent volunteers with knowledge as to how to deal with power structures and a sense of commitment concerning what they do. There are obviously many other trends and possibilities which might be in evidence; this has been a best-case scenario. It is exciting to ponder the possibilities of the mixture of the old wine of experience with the new wine evident a few years away.

NOTES

1. Tonnies, Ferdinand. *Community and Society* (Charles F. Loonies, translator and editor) (New York: Harper and Row, 1963).

2. Goffman, Erving. "Characteristics of Total Institutions." In *Identity and Anxiety: Survival of the Person in Mass Society.* Maurice R. Stein, Arthur Vidisk, and David M. White (eds.) (New York: Free Press, 1960).

3. Goode, William J. "Community Within a Community: The Professions." *American Sociological Review,*